MW00353718

The Gray
and the
Blue

The *Gray* and the **Blue**

A COMIC STRIP HISTORY OF THE CIVIL WAR

Charles H. Hayes

PELICAN PUBLISHING COMPANY

Gretna 2011

Copyright © 2011
By Charles H. Hayes
All rights reserved

The word "Pelican" and the depiction of a pelican are
trademarks of Pelican Publishing Company, Inc. and are
registered in the U.S. Patent and Trademark Office.

ISBN: 978-1-58980-967-3

Printed in the United States of America

Published by Pelican Publishing Company, Inc.
1000 Burmaster Street, Gretna, Louisiana 70053

To my great-grandfather
Ephraim T. Hayes
Sixth Ohio Volunteer Cavalry
who fought to restore the Union

and

my great-grandfather
Joseph D. Howe
Twentieth Mississippi Infantry
who fought for Southern Independence

Neither of these soldiers owned slaves although,
throughout the entire war, slavery was legal in both the
Confederate States of America and the United States
of America.

—Charles Howe Hayes

Contents

CHAPTER 1

CAUSES
Why Did the War Occur?

4 JULY 1776

ORIGINALLY THE WORDS <u>STATE</u> AND <u>NATION</u> HAD THE SAME MEANING.

His majesty acknowledges the said United States, viz., New Hampshire, Massachusetts Bay, Rhode Island and Providence Plantations, Connecticut, New York, New Jersey, Pennsylvania, Delaware, Maryland, Virginia, North Carolina, South Carolina, and Georgia, to be FREE, SOVEREIGN AND INDEPENDENT STATES. He treats with them as such.

George III

SEPTEMBER 3, 1783

IN THE TREATY ENDING THE AMERICAN REVOLUTION, KING GEORGE RECOGNIZED EACH OF THE THIRTEEN COLONIES AS AN INDEPENDENT STATE (NATION).

THE ORIGINAL THIRTEEN STATES REGARDED THEMSELVES AS SOVEREIGN NATIONS, AND THE CONSTITUTION AS A COMPACT AMONG THEM.

IN RATIFYING THE CONSTITUTION. VIRGINIA. NEW YORK. AND RHODE ISLAND ALL RESERVED THE RIGHT TO WITHDRAW.

THE CONSTITUTION USED THE PLURAL, AND CORRECT GRAMMAR REQUIRED THE SAME FORM.

One by one the northern states had done away with slavery, but without freeing the slaves.

JUNE 1, 1796
After the Constitution was adopted by the original 13 states, new states were admitted as free or slave without much argument.

But in 1819, when Missouri petitioned for admission as a slave state there was considerable argument.

After much debate, a compromise was worked out and Missouri was admitted as a slave state.

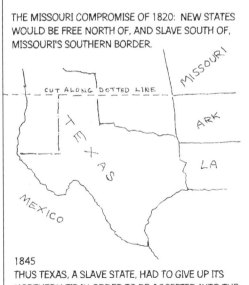

The Missouri Compromise of 1820: New states would be free north of, and slave south of, Missouri's southern border.

CUT ALONG DOTTED LINE

MISSOURI

TEXAS

ARK

LA

MEXICO

1845
Thus Texas, a slave state, had to give up its northern tip in order to be accepted into the Union.

Texas, like the original thirteen states, had been an independent nation, and, in its treaty of annexation, retained the explicit right to withdraw.

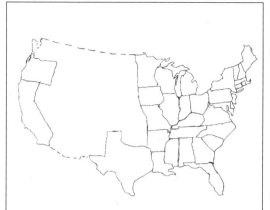

BUT NEW STATES WERE ADDED THAT HAD NEVER BEEN INDEPENDENT NATIONS, AND MILLIONS OF IMMIGRANTS, IGNORANT OF THE FOUNDING PRINCIPLES OF THE UNION, ARRIVED. FOR MANY THE MEANING OF **STATE** BEGAN TO LOSE THE IDEA OF **NATION.**

THE WHIG PARTY DISINTEGRATED UNDER THE PRESSURE OF THE SLAVERY QUESTION.

1854 - MEMBERS OF THE FREE SOIL PARTY ALONG WITH NORTHERN WHIGS, ABOLITIONISTS, AND ANTI-SLAVERY DEMOCRATS MEET TO FOUND A NEW POLITICAL PARTY.

THE ROLE OF RACISM

Racism was not an issue. It is true that the white people of the South thought that their race was superior to any other on earth. The great majority of northern whites felt the same way, and so did Englishmen and other Europeans.

They would feel this way long after the War for Southern Independence was over, well into the twentieth century.

WHY THE REPUBLICANS OPPOSED SLAVERY IN THE TERRITORIES

"...All unoccupied territory of the United States, and such as they may hereafter acquire, shall be reserved for the white Caucasian race--a thing that cannot be except by the exclusion of slavery."

----From the 1856 Republican Presidential Platform

1850
BUT WHEN CALIFORNIA PETITIONED FOR ADMISSION AS A FREE STATE, THE NORTH RENEGED ON THE MISSOURI COMPROMISE.

THE KANSAS-NEBRASKA ACT OF 1854

ALTHOUGH NORTH OF THE 1820 COMPROMISE LINE, KANSAS WOULD DECIDE BY VOTE WHETHER IT WOULD BECOME A SLAVE OR A FREE STATE.

PRO- AND ANTISLAVERY SETTLERS RUSHED INTO KANSAS IN A RACE TO FORM A MAJORITY.

MAY 1856
POTTAWATOMIE CREEK, KANSAS

JOHN BROWN'S GANG HACKS FARMER DOYLE AND HIS FOUR SONS TO DEATH WITH SWORDS.

DESPITE THESE MURDERS, BROWN WAS SHELTERED IN BOSTON BY RESPECTED ABOLITIONISTS, INCLUDING MINISTERS.

1857
IN THE DRED SCOTT CASE, THE U.S. SUPREME COURT RULED THAT SLAVE OWNERS, WITH THEIR SLAVES, COULD NOT BE KEPT OUT OF ANY TERRITORY. NEVERTHELESS, THE REPUBLICANS CONTINUED TO CAMPAIGN ON THIS ISSUE.

1858 - THE NEW PARTY, MADE UP ALMOST ENTIRELY OF ANTISLAVERY NORTHERNERS, MAKES SURPRISING GAINS IN THE CONGRESSIONAL ELECTIONS.

WHY THE SOUTH THOUGHT SLAVERY MUST BE PERMITTED IN THE TERRITORIES.

THE NIGHT OF OCTOBER 16, 1859

SECRETLY FINANCED BY PROMINENT MASSACHUSETTS ABOLITIONISTS, BROWN AND 21 ARMED HENCHMEN, BLACK AND WHITE, ENTER HARPERS FERRY, VIRGINIA.

THEY EASILY CAPTURED THE U.S. ARSENAL.

THEY ROUNDED UP THE TOWN'S LEADING CITZENS AS HOSTAGES.

BROWN SENT BLACK MEMBERS OF HIS BAND INTO THE COUNTRYSIDE TO ARM THE SLAVES.

FAILING TO RECRUIT ANYONE, BROWN'S MEN WISELY RETURNED NORTH WITHOUT REPORTING BACK TO HARPERS FERRY.

AT DAWN THE LOCAL MILITIA OPENED FIRE AND KEPT BROWN'S GANG PINNED DOWN UNTIL A COMPANY OF U.S. MARINES ARRIVED.

12

HOLDING THEIR FIRE TO AVOID HITTING THE HOSTAGES THE MARINES, COMMANDED BY COL. ROBERT E. LEE, CHARGED WITH BAYONETTES AND A BATTERING RAM.

BROWN AND THE FEW SURVIVING MEMBERS OF HIS GANG WERE CAPTURED. THE HOSTAGES WERE UNHARMED BUT DURING THEIR STAY IN HARPERS FERRY, THE GANG HAD KILLED THE MAYOR, A MARINE, AND A FREE BLACK.

BROWN WAS TRIED IN A STATE COURT FOR TREASON AGAINST VIRGINIA. HE WAS CONVICTED AND ON DECEMBER 2, 1859 HE WAS HANGED.

BROWN WAS PRAISED IN MANY NORTHERN NEWSPAPERS, AND SPECIAL CHURCH SERVICES WERE HELD ALL OVER NEW ENGLAND. THE SOUTH WAS SHOCKED MORE BY THE NORTH'S REACTION THAN BY WHAT BROWN HAD DONE.

The U.S. CONSTITUTION
Article 4, Section 2, Clause 3

"*No person held to service or labor in one state, under the laws thereof, escaping into another, shall, in consequence of any law or regulation therein, be discharged from such service or labor, but shall be delivered up on claim of the party to whom such service or labor may be due.*"

STATES CONTROLLED BY THE REPUBLICANS WERE NO LONGER FULFILLING THEIR OBLIGATION UNDER THE U.S. CONSTITUTION TO RETURN ESCAPED SLAVES.

THE SOUTH WAS FED UP WITH REPUBLICANS.

MOST SOUTHERNERS DID NOT OWN SLAVES, BUT THEY RESENTED OUTSIDERS FORCING CHANGES ON THEM.

TAXES ON IMPORTS AND EXPORTS

BECAUSE THEY WERE FARTHER FROM THE NORTHERN FACTORIES, SOUTHERNERS DID MOST OF THE TRADING WITH FOREIGN COUNTRIES. TARIFFS WERE THE MAIN SOURCE OF ALL U.S. GOVERNMENT INCOME, SO SOUTHERNERS SAW THEMSELVES AS THE MAIN SUPPORT OF A GOVERNMENT THAT SEEMED TO CARE LESS AND LESS ABOUT THEM.

IN ADDITION TO PROVIDING REVENUE, THE TARIFFS PROTECTED NORTHERN MANUFACTURERS FROM FOREIGN COMPETITION.

LINCOLN'S "HOUSE DIVIDED" SPEECH SOUNDED TO SOUTHERNERS LIKE A WAR THREAT.

SLAVERY AGITATION WILL NOT CEASE UNTIL *A CRISIS SHALL HAVE BEEN REACHED AND PASSED.* A HOUSE DIVIDED AGAINST ITSELF CANNOT STAND. *I BELIEVE THIS GOVERNMENT CANNOT ENDURE HALF SLAVE AND HALF FREE.* I DO NOT EXPECT THE UNION TO BE DISSOLVED -- I DO NOT EXPECT THE HOUSE TO FALL -- BUT I DO EXPECT IT WILL CEASE TO BE DIVIDED. *IT WILL BECOME ALL ONE THING,* OR ALL THE OTHER.

Abraham Lincoln
June 16, 1858

NOVEMBER 1860 -- THE SOUTH IS STUNNED TO LEARN THAT THE REPUBLICAN CANDIDATE, ABE LINCOLN, HAS BEEN ELECTED PRESIDENT.

DECEMBER 3, 1860
WHEN CONGRESS CONVENES AFTER THE ELECTIONS THERE ARE TWO SENATORS MISSING.

SECESSION HALL, CHARLESTON

DECEMBER 17, 1860
SOUTH CAROLINA CALLS A CONVENTION TO CONSIDER AN ORDINANCE OF SECESSION.

THE CONVENTION PASSED A MOMENTOUS RESOLUTION.

SOUTHERN DOMINOES

THE SIX SOUTHERNMOST STATES RAPIDLY FOLLOW SOUTH CAROLINA IN SECEDING.

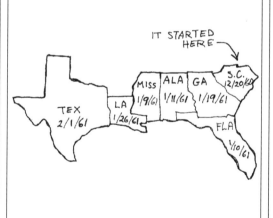

THESE SEVEN STATES WILL FORM THE ORIGINAL CONFEDERATE STATES OF AMERICA.

DID THE STATES SECEDE SO THAT THEY COULD KEEP SLAVERY?

No. They didn't have to. Slavery could be ended only by amending the Constitution, which required approval of three-fourths of the states. The fact that there were fifteen slave states made this impossible.

The slavery argument leading to secession was about slavery in the territories, not in the states.

JANUARY, 1861
DELEGATES FROM THE SEVEN SECEDED STATES MEET IN MONTGOMERY, ALABAMA, TO FORM A NEW UNION, THE CONFEDERATE STATES OF AMERICA.

JEFFERSON DAVIS

THE DELEGATES CHOOSE THE RECENTLY RESIGNED U.S. SENATOR FROM MISSISSIPPI AS PRESIDENT.

DAVIS, A GRADUATE OF WEST POINT AND A VETERAN OF THE MEXICAN WAR, WOULD RATHER HAVE COMMANDED AN ARMY.

THE STARS AND BARS

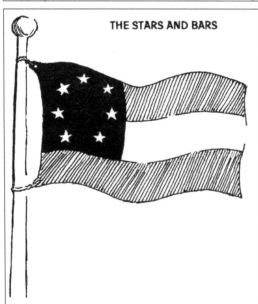

THE NEW FLAG - SEVEN STARS FOR THE STATES OF S. CAROLINA, GEORGIA, FLORIDA, MISSISSIPPI, LOUISIANA, ALABAMA, AND TEXAS.

TEXAS GOVERNOR SAM HOUSTON REFUSES TO SWEAR ALLEGIANCE TO THE CONFEDERACY, AND IS FORCIBLY REMOVED FROM HIS OFFICE.

THE CONFEDERACY WAS FORMED DURING THE FINAL MONTHS OF THE BUCHANAN PRESIDENCY.

JAMES BUCHANAN - 15th PRESIDENT
DEMOCRAT FROM PENNSYLVANIA

AS THE STATES SECEDED, THEY WANTED THE U.S. TO GIVE OR SELL BACK THE FORTS AND POST OFFICES THEY HAD PREVIOUSLY GIVEN OR SOLD TO THE FEDERAL GOVERNMENT.

PRESIDENT BUCHANAN MADE A PRACTICAL DECISION.

CHANGING THE POST OFFICES WAS EASY.

MOST OF THE FORTS WERE IN WEST TEXAS.

THE CONFEDERACY SENT COMMISSIONERS TO WASHINGTON TO NEGOTIATE RELEASING THE REMAINING FORTS.

PRESIDENT BUCHANAN AGREED TO MEET WITH THE SOUTHERN COMMISSIONERS UNOFFICIALLY.

BUCHANAN WAS TORN BETWEEN TWO CONFLICTING CONVICTIONS...

SO HE PASSED THE PROBLEM ON TO THE INCOMING LINCOLN ADMINISTRATION.

DID THE STATES HAVE THE RIGHT TO SECEDE?

WE HAVE SEEN HOW THE ARGUMENTS OVER SLAVERY LED SOME OF THE STATES TO SECEDE. NOW THERE WOULD BE A WAR, NOT OVER SLAVERY, BUT OVER SECESSION.

WAS SECESSION LAWFUL? LINCOLN NEVER ASKED THE SUPREME COURT FOR A RULING.

CAUSES for SECESSION OR CAUSES for WAR?

Slavery, regional differences in outlook, and tariffs are usually cited as causes for the war. They were not; they were causes for secession. The war was caused by Lincoln's refusal to allow the southern states to withdraw peaceably from the union.

CHAPTER 2

FORT SUMTER
The Fighting Starts

THE MAIN FORTIFICATIONS AT CHARLESTON

THE U.S. OFFICER IN COMMAND:

MAJOR ROBERT ANDERSON

THE OTHER FORTS WERE VULNERABLE TO ATTACK BY LAND, SO HE DECIDED TO MOVE EVERYONE TO FORT SUMTER.

HE ORDERED THE FORT MOULTRIE GUNS SPIKED AND THEIR CARRIAGES BURNED.

HE EVEN HAD THE REVOLUTIONARY WAR FLAG MAST CHOPPED DOWN AND BURNED.

DEC. 26, 1860 - IN THE DARK OF NIGHT MAJOR ANDERSON MOVES THE EIGHTY MAN FORT MOULTRIE COMMAND TO FORT SUMTER.

CHARLESTON WAS SURPRISED THE NEXT DAWN TO SEE THE STARS AND STRIPES RAISED AT FORT SUMTER.

GENERAL PIERRE BEAUREGARD

MARCH 1, 1861 - PRESIDENT DAVIS ORDERS GEN. BEAUREGARD TO TAKE COMMAND OF OPERATIONS IN CHARLESTON.

GENERAL BEAUREGARD HAD THE CANNONS AT FORT MOULTRIE REPAIRED AND REMOUNTED.

AT ANOTHER STRATEGIC SPOT HE BUILT A HIDDEN BATTERY BEHIND A ROW OF HOUSES

MARCH 4, 1861 - THE NATION WONDERS IF LINCOLN'S INAUGURAL SPEECH WILL TRY TO APPEASE THE SECEDED STATES.

BUT THE SUPREME COURT HAD DECIDED THAT SLAVERY MUST ALSO BE ALLOWED IN THE TERRITORIES.

He denied the right to secede.

He was ready to fight to hold Ft. Sumter.

Unlike Buchanan, Lincoln refused to see the Confederate Commissioners.

After Lincoln's inaugural address and his rebuff of the Confederate Commissioners, Fort Sumter became the focus of attention in both the North and the South.

Everyone knew that war could break out over this touchy issue.

Lincoln was determined not to surrender the fort, and Davis was just as determined not to allow the federals to reinforce it.

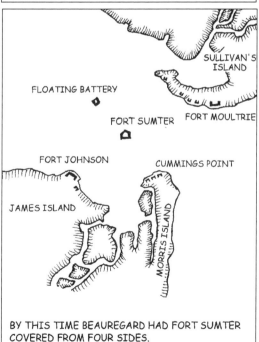

By this time Beauregard had Fort Sumter covered from four sides.

General Beauregard tried to starve Anderson's command into surrender.

MAJOR ANDERSON CALLED A CONFERENCE WITH THE OTHER OFFICERS.

THINGS WERE LOOKING BLEAK.

BACK IN WASHINGTON - SEWARD SENT WORD THAT FORT SUMTER WOULD NOT BE REINFORCED...

BUT TROOP TRANSPORTS WERE ALREADY ON THE WAY.

WHEN PRESIDENT DAVIS LEARNED THAT RE-INFORCEMENTS WERE ON THE WAY, HE ORDERED BEAUREGARD TO OBTAIN ANDERSON'S SURRENDER OR TO REDUCE THE FORT.

I have the honor to acknowledge the receipt of your communication demanding the evacuation of this fort...
It is a demand with which I regret that my sense of honor and of my obligation to my Government prevent my compliance.

Robert Anderson

BEAUREGARD RECEIVED HIS ANSWER.

APRIL 12, 1861, 4:30 AM -
THE "HONOR" OF FIRING THE FIRST SHOT IS OFFERED TO ROGER PRYOR, AN OUTSPOKEN ADVOCATE FOR THE ATTACK.

AWED BY THE RESPONSIBILITY, PRYOR PASSED THE DUTY TO EDMUND RUFFIN, A "FIRE-EATER" PUBLISHER OF A FARM MAGAZINE.

EDMUND RUFFIN

ALTHOUGH RUFFIN IS GENERALLY CREDITED WITH FIRING THE FIRST SHOT OF THE CIVIL WAR...

THERE WAS A "FIRST SHOT" FIRED FROM EACH OF THE CONFEDERATE BATTERIES SURROUNDING FORT SUMTER.

AT ONE OF THE BATTERIES THAT DISTINCTION WAS OFFERED TO SOUTH CAROLINA GOVERNOR FRANCIS PICKENS.

PICKENS HELPED HIS SMALL DAUGHTER EUGENIA "DOUSCHKA" PICKENS YANK THE FIRING LANYARD.

THE CONFEDERATE CANNONADE WAS DEVASTATING.

SOME OF THE CONFEDERATE GUNS WERE LOADED WITH HOT SHOT.

FORT SUMTER STOPS RETURNING THE REBEL FIRE.

FINALLY A FEW SHOTS COME FROM SUMTER-- AND THE REBELS CHEER.

THAT NIGHT, AT ONE OF THE GUN CASEMENTS...

DURING THE BATTLE ANDERSON RECEIVES A STRANGE VISIT.

24

YOU TOOK A TERRIBLE RISK, SENATOR, WITH ALL THAT REBEL FIRE HITTING IN THE AREA.

THEY AIN'T HITTING THE AREA, MAJOR. EVERY SHOT IS LANDING IN THE FORT.

WITHOUT ANY OFFICIAL CAPACITY, WIGFALL NEGOTIATES TERMS OF SURRENDER.

BOOM! BOOM! BOOM!

BEFORE EVACUATING FT. SUMTER, ANDERSON ORDERS A 100 GUN SALUTE TO THE FLAG.

THE CANNON FIRING THE 50TH SHOT EXPLODES, KILLING ONE MAN AND INJURING FIVE, THE ONLY CASUALTIES OF THE BATTLE.

HE'S THE FIRST OF GOD KNOWS HOW MANY MORE TO COME.

THE DEAD MAN WAS PRIVATE DANIEL HOUGH, THE FIRST FATALITY OF THE WAR.

CHAPTER 3

MANASSAS
The First Big Battle

AFTER THE ATTACK ON FORT SUMTER, LINCOLN AND HIS CABINET CONSIDER THE NEXT MOVE.

YOU'LL HAVE TO CALL CONGRESS INTO SESSION TO DECLARE WAR.

NO I WON'T. THIS ISN'T WAR IT'S INSURRECTION.

I'M ISSUING A PROCLAMATION CALLING FOR 75,000 VOLUNTEERS FOR 3 MONTHS.

GOVERNMENT BY PROCLAMATION BEGINS.

TENNESSEE WILL FURNISH NOT A SINGLE MAN FOR THE PURPOSE OF COERCION, BUT FIFTY THOUSAND IF NECESSARY FOR THE DEFENSE OF OUR RIGHTS AND THOSE OF OUR SOUTHERN BROTHERS.

Isham G. Harris

THE GOVERNOR OF TENNESSEE SUMMED UP THE GENERAL RESENTMENT OF THE BORDER STATES TO LINCOLN'S CALL FOR MEN TO INVADE SOUTH CAROLINA.

YOU CAN'T ARREST ME. I'M A STATE SENATOR.

YEAH, BUT YOU'D VOTE TO SECEDE.

LINCOLN USED THE ARMY TO MAKE SURE THAT MARYLAND REMAINED IN THE UNION.

THE CONFEDERACY AS SEEN BY THE NORTH:

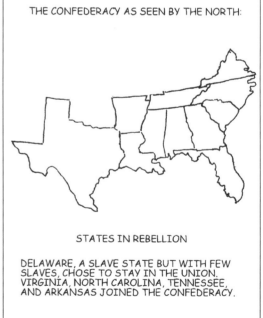

STATES IN REBELLION

DELAWARE, A SLAVE STATE BUT WITH FEW SLAVES, CHOSE TO STAY IN THE UNION. VIRGINIA, NORTH CAROLINA, TENNESSEE, AND ARKANSAS JOINED THE CONFEDERACY.

THE CONFEDERACY AS SEEN BY THE SOUTH:

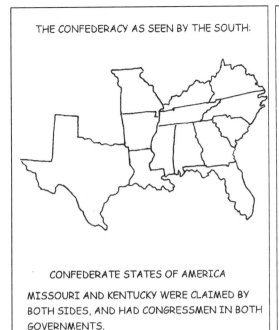

CONFEDERATE STATES OF AMERICA

MISSOURI AND KENTUCKY WERE CLAIMED BY BOTH SIDES, AND HAD CONGRESSMEN IN BOTH GOVERNMENTS.

THE STARS AND BARS

THE CONFEDERATE FLAG NOW HAD THIRTEEN STARS.

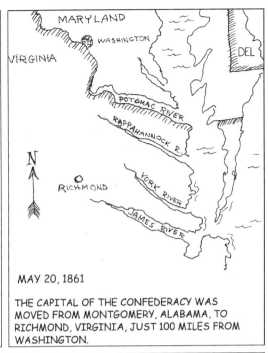

MAY 20, 1861

THE CAPITAL OF THE CONFEDERACY WAS MOVED FROM MONTGOMERY, ALABAMA, TO RICHMOND, VIRGINIA, JUST 100 MILES FROM WASHINGTON.

LINCOLN'S GENERAL-IN-CHIEF WAS WINFIELD SCOTT, FAMOUS FROM THE MEXICAN WAR BUT NOW TOO OLD TO LEAD TROOPS IN COMBAT.

WE'LL TAKE CONTROL OF THE MISSISSIPPI AND BLOCKADE ALL THEIR PORTS.

IT LOOKS LIKE A GIANT SNAKE!

GENERAL SCOTT NOW LAID OUT A LONG TERM STRATEGY.

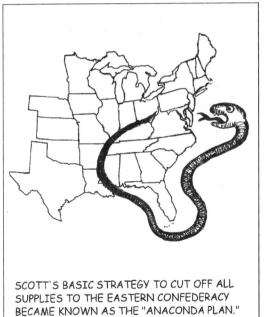

SCOTT'S BASIC STRATEGY TO CUT OFF ALL SUPPLIES TO THE EASTERN CONFEDERACY BECAME KNOWN AS THE "ANACONDA PLAN."

SCOTT THOUGHT HIS STRATEGIC "ANACONDA" PLAN WOULD FORCE THE SOUTH BACK INTO THE UNION WITH THE LEAST LOSS OF LIFE ON BOTH SIDES. LINCOLN BEGAN TO PUT SCOTT'S PLAN INTO EFFECT BY DECLARING A BLOCKADE ON ALL CONFEDERATE PORTS.

BUT LINCOLN INSISTED ON AN IMMEDIATE MARCH ON THE SOUTHERN CAPITAL, RICHMOND, VIRGINIA.

75,000 MEN AND THREE MONTHS AREN'T ENOUGH. WE'LL NEED 300,000 MEN, THREE YEARS, AND THE BEST OFFICERS.

I REGRET THAT VIRGINIA LEFT THE UNION, BUT MY DUTY IS TO MY HOME STATE.

SCOTT WANTED ROBERT E. LEE AS FIELD COMMANDER OF THE U.S. ARMY.

WELL, JOHNSTON, CAN I COUNT ON YOU?

I CAN'T LIFT MY SWORD AGAINST TEXAS.

SCOTT'S SECOND CHOICE, ALBERT SIDNEY JOHNSTON, ALSO TURNED HIM DOWN.

GENERAL IRVIN McDOWELL

SCOTT DELEGATED THE COMMAND OF THE INVADING ARMY TO GEN. McDOWELL.

JUST ONE MORE WATERMELLON AND I'LL CALL IT QUITS.

(IF HE FIGHTS LIKE HE EATS WE'LL BE IN GOOD SHAPE.)

McDOWELL WAS FAMOUS AS A GOURMAND.

THE COMPANY

AT FULL STRENGTH THE COMPANY COMPRISED 100 MEN AS FOLLOWS

1 CAPTAIN
1 FIRST LIEUTENANT
1 SECOND LIEUTENANT
1 FIRST SERGEANT
4 SERGEANTS
8 CORPORALS
84 PRIVATES

CONFEDERATE UNITS AVERAGED ONLY HALF STRENGTH, 50 MEN TO A COMPANY, ETC.

THE REGIMENT

AT FULL STRENGTH THE REGIMENT COMPRISED 10 COMPANIES WITH A TOTAL OF 1000 MEN

REGIMENTAL OFFICERS:
- 1 COLONEL
- 1 LIEUTENANT COLONEL
- 1 MAJOR
- 1 ADJUTANT (LIEUTENANT)
- 1 QUARTER MASTER (LIEUTENANT)
- 2 SURGEONS

REGIMENTAL NONCOMMISSIONED OFFICERS
- 1 SERGEANT MAJOR
- 1 QUARTERMASTER SERGEANT
- 1 COMMISSARY SERGEANT
- 1 HOSPITAL STEWARD

THE BRIGADE
TWO OR MORE REGIMENTS OF THE SAME TYPE, FOR EXAMPLE, INFANTRY.
COMMANDER: BRIGADIER GENERAL (ONE STAR)

THE DIVISION
SEVERAL REGIMENTS OF DIFFERENT TYPES, FOR EXAMPLE, INFANTRY, CAVALRY, ARTILLERY.
COMMANDER: MAJOR GENERAL (TWO STARS)

THE CORPS
SEVERAL DIVISIONS.
COMMANDER: MAJOR GENERAL (TWO STARS)

THE ARMY
SEVERAL CORPS.
COMMANDER: MAJOR GENERAL OR
LIEUTENANT GENERAL (THREE STARS)

GENERALS WERE APPOINTED BY THE PRESIDENTS..

COLONELS WERE APPOINTED BY THE GOVERNORS.

JULY 21, 1861
THE TWO ARMIES MEET FOR THE FIRST MAJOR BATTLE AT MANASSAS JUNCTION, VIRGINIA.

MANY OF WASHINGTON'S HIGH SOCIETY RODE OUT IN CARRIAGES TO WITNESS THE SQUASHING OF THE "REBELLION."

AT FIRST IT SEEMED TO BE A GREAT VICTORY FOR THE NORTH.

THE RETREATING SOUTHERNERS WERE EN-COURAGED BY ONE BRIGADE THAT REFUSED TO WITHDRAW.

GENERAL THOMAS J. JACKSON

KNOWN AFTER MANASSAS AS "STONEWALL" JACKSON

WHAT AT FIRST SEEMED A GREAT VICTORY FOR THE UNION SOON TURNED INTO AN INGLORIOUS ROUT.

PICNICKING DIGNITARIES ALONG WITH COMMON SOLDIERS WERE ALL CAUGHT UP IN A PANIC TO GET BACK TO WASHINGTON.

WHEN THE EXHAUSTED AND FRIGHTENED SURVIVORS OF HIS ARMY BEGAN ARRIVING IN WASHINGTON, LINCOLN REALIZED THAT THE "INSURRECTION" WOULD BE A LONG AND HAZARDOUS WAR.

★★★

THE SOUTHERNERS FAILED TO PURSUE THE VANQUISHED YANKEES INTO WASHINGTON. IF THEY HAD, THE CITY COULD POSSIBLY HAVE BEEN CAPTURED AND THE WAR WON.

THERE HAD BEEN MUCH CONFUSION DUE TO THE VARIED UNIFORMS IN BOTH ARMIES.

THE SIMILARITY OF THE NATIONAL FLAGS ALSO CAUSED CONFUSION.

ONE BATTERY HAD BEEN WIPED OUT BECAUSE ATTACKING REBELS WERE MISTAKEN FOR REINFORCING YANKS.

GENERAL BEAUREGARD DESIGNED A NEW BATTLE FLAG TO REDUCE FUTURE CONFUSION.

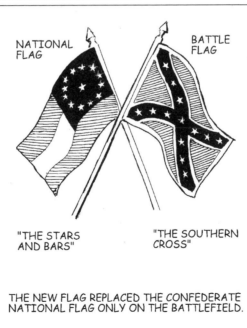

THE NEW FLAG REPLACED THE CONFEDERATE NATIONAL FLAG ONLY ON THE BATTLEFIELD.

JULY 25, 1861
THE UNITED STATES SENATE FORMALLY DECLARES THAT THE WAR AGAINST THE SOUTH IS FOR THE PURPOSE OF PRESERVING THE UNION, AND NOT FOR ENDING SLAVERY.

CHAPTER 4

NASHVILLE
The South Loses a Key City

GENERAL GEORGE B. McCLELLAN

LINCOLN RELIEVED McDOWELL AND GAVE HIS DISPIRITED ARMY TO YOUNG GENERAL McCLELLAN TO REORGANIZE AND TRAIN.

HUP! TWO! THREE! FOUR!

I CALL IT THE ARMY OF THE POTOMAC.

McCLELLAN SHOWED AMAZING ABILITY IN TRAINING THE ARMY AND REVIVING ITS SPIRIT.

WHEN ARE YOU GOING TO MARCH ON RICHMOND?

SOON, MR. PRESIDENT, SOON.

THE ARMY OF THE POTOMAC GREW TO OVER 150,000 BUT McCLELLAN NEVER THOUGHT IT WAS PREPARED ENOUGH TO FIGHT.

WHILE McCLELLAN SLOWLY PREPARED FOR ANOTHER INVASION OF VIRGINIA, THE SCENE OF ACTION SHIFTED WESTWARD.

YOU'RE MY BEST GENERAL, SO I'M GIVING YOU THE TOUGHEST JOB!

THANKS! (I GUESS.)

OF ALL THE CONFEDERATE GENERALS PRESIDENT DAVIS HAD THE MOST CONFIDENCE IN ALBERT SIDNEY JOHNSTON. DAVIS PUT HIM IN CHARGE OF A REGION STRETCHING FROM KENTUCKY TO THE INDIAN TERRITORY.

GEN. ALBERT SIDNEY JOHNSTON, CSA

JOHNSTON SERVED IN THREE ARMIES: THE REPUBLIC OF TEXAS, THE UNITED STATES OF AMERICA, AND NOW THE CONFEDERATE STATES OF AMERICA.

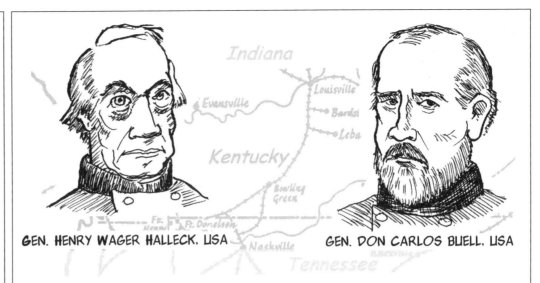

GEN. HENRY WAGER HALLECK, USA

GEN. DON CARLOS BUELL, USA

THE U.S. FORCES OPPOSING JOHNSTON WERE DIVIDED BETWEEN TWO COMMANDERS, EACH HAVING MORE MEN THAN JOHNSTON.

I'VE GOT GENERAL ZOLLICOFFER GUARDING THE CUMBERLAND GAP.

ZOLLICOFFER IS INEXPERIENCED. BETTER GO CHECK TO SEE IF HE IS IN A GOOD DEFENSIVE POSITION.

JOHNSTON PLACED GENERAL GEORGE B. CRITTENDEN IN CHARGE OF THE EASTERN END OF HIS LINE.

YOU'VE PLACED YOUR COMMAND IN A TRAP WITH YOUR BACK TO THE RIVER!!

THERE WEREN'T ANY GOOD CAMP SITES ON THE SOUTH SIDE.

TO HIS DISMAY, CRITTENDEN FOUND ZOLLICOFFER ENCAMPED ON THE WRONG SIDE OF THE CUMBERLAND.

IF WE MARCH ALL NIGHT WE CAN SURPRISE THEM AT DAWN!

ZOLLIE, YOU TALKED ME INTO IT!

BEFORE CRITTENDEN COULD MOVE THE CAMP, WORD CAME THAT THE YANKEES WERE APPROACHING. ALTHOUGH OUTNUMBERED, THEY DECIDED TO STRIKE FIRST.

IN A HEAVY RAIN, THE CONFEDERATE TROOPS SLOGGED ALL NIGHT ALONG MUDDY ROADS.

19 JANUARY 1862
MILL SPRINGS, KENTUCKY

AT DAWN THE REBELS ATTACKED.

THE CONFEDERATE ATTACK FALTERED WHEN SOME OF THEIR MUSKETS FAILED TO FIRE.

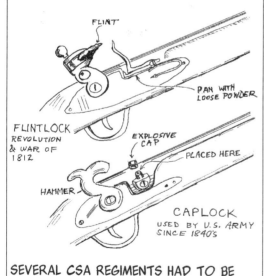

SEVERAL CSA REGIMENTS HAD TO BE WITHDRAWN FROM THE FIGHT BECAUSE THEIR ANTIQUATED FLINTLOCK MUSKETS WOULDN'T WORK IN THE DRIVING RAIN.

IN THE RAIN NEARSIGHTED GEN. ZOLLICOFFER MISTOOK A UNION COLONEL FOR ONE OF HIS OWN OFFICERS.

ZOLLICOFFER'S DEATH WAS THE LAST STRAW. THE DEMORALIZED SOUTHERNERS RETREATED, AND THE RETREAT BECAME A ROUT.

AS CRITTENDEN'S BROKEN ARMY RETREATED TOWARD NASHVILLE, PRESIDENT DAVIS SENT GENERAL BEAUREGARD TO ASSIST JOHNSTON.

GENERAL ULYSSES S. GRANT

NOW GENERAL HALLECK BEGAN HIS ATTACK BY SENDING HIS MOST AGGRESSIVE GENERAL INTO WESTERN TENNESSEE.

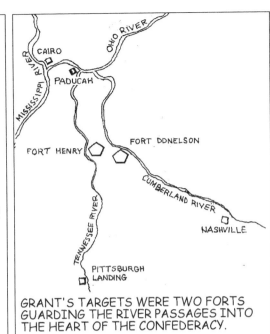

GRANT'S TARGETS WERE TWO FORTS GUARDING THE RIVER PASSAGES INTO THE HEART OF THE CONFEDERACY.

THE COMBINED U.S. LAND AND RIVER FORCES FIRST APPROACHED FORT HENRY. IT WAS BEING FLOODED BY THE FAST-RISING TENNESEE RIVER.

6 FEBRUARY 1862

C.S. GENERAL TILGHMAN CHOSE A SACRIFICE COMPANY TO HOLD THE FORT WHILE THE REST OF THE BRIGADE ESCAPED TOWARD FORT DONELSON.

THE REBELS WERE ABLE TO DAMAGE SEVERAL GUNBOATS BEFORE THE ENEMY FIRE AND THE RISING RIVER CLAIMED MOST OF THEIR GUNS.

BY THIS TIME THE WATER HAD RISEN HIGH ENOUGH FOR THE FLAGSHIP TO DOCK AT THE FORT RAMPARTS.

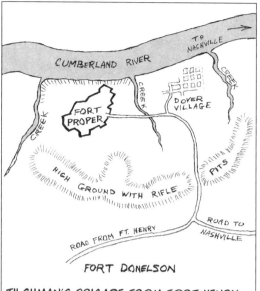

TILGHMAN'S BRIGADE FROM FORT HENRY BROUGHT THE FORT DONELSON GARRISON UP TO 13,000.

THE TROUBLE WAS THE GENERALS.

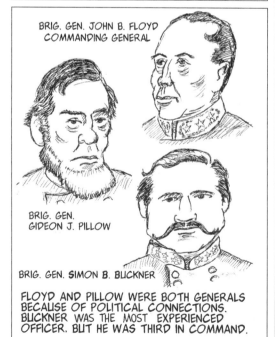

BRIG. GEN. JOHN B. FLOYD COMMANDING GENERAL

BRIG. GEN. GIDEON J. PILLOW

BRIG. GEN. SIMON B. BUCKNER

FLOYD AND PILLOW WERE BOTH GENERALS BECAUSE OF POLITICAL CONNECTIONS. BUCKNER WAS THE MOST EXPERIENCED OFFICER, BUT HE WAS THIRD IN COMMAND.

THE FIRST ASSAULT BY THE U.S. LAND FORCES WAS TURNED BACK WITH HEAVY LOSSES.

THE FIRST ATTACK BY THE UNION GUNBOATS ALSO FAILED.

GENERAL FLOYD IS OUT OF DANGER!

GREAT! TELL HIM TO WITHDRAW TO NASHVILLE BEFORE THE YANKEES RECOVER.

GEN. FLOYD SENT A TELEGRAM TO JOHNSTON ANNOUNCING A COMPLETE VICTORY.

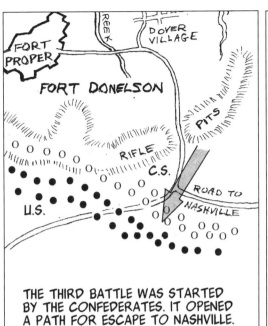

THE THIRD BATTLE WAS STARTED BY THE CONFEDERATES. IT OPENED A PATH FOR ESCAPE TO NASHVILLE.

GEN. BUCKNER. GEN. FLOYD SAYS TO WITHDRAW INTO THE FORT!

?? BUT WE'VE JUST OPENED THE WAY OUT!!

BUT PILLOW DECIDED AT THE LAST MOMENT NOT TO EVACUATE. SO FLOYD ORDERED EVERYONE BACK INTO THE FORT.

ALAS AND ALACK!

WOE IS US!

THAT IT SHOULD COME TO THIS!

THAT NIGHT, FEELING THAT THEY HAD MISSED THEIR ONE CHANCE TO ESCAPE, THE THREE GENERALS CONCLUDED THAT THEY HAD TO SURRENDER.

I PASS THE COMMAND TO PILLOW.

I PASS IT TO BUCKNER.

I ACCEPT IT. I'LL ASK GRANT FOR TERMS.

NEITHER FLOYD NOR PILLOW WANTED TO BE TAKEN PRISONER, SO THEY PASSED THE COMMAND TO BUCKNER AND PREPARED TO LEAVE THE FORT BY BOAT.

I DIDN'T BRING MY COMMAND HERE TO SURRENDER IT!

ONE CAVALRY COLONEL PRESENT AT THE CONFERENCE STRONGLY OBJECTED TO THE SURRENDER.

NATHAN BEDFORD FORREST. CSA FORREST. A RICH MISSISSIPPI PLANTER, HAD RECRUITED HIS OWN REGIMENT AND OUT-FITTED IT WITH HIS OWN MONEY.

EASY, HORSE! I KNOW THAT WATER'S COLD.

OLD FORREST WILL GET US THROUGH.

FORREST LED HIS MEN TO FREEDOM THROUGH THE ICY WATERS OF AN UNGUARDED SLOUGH. THE YANKEES WOULD HEAR FROM HIM AGAIN.

WHAT?! WE WHIPPED THE YANKEES THREE TIMES.

AND WE COULD DO IT AGAIN!

THE MEN OF FORT DONELSON COULD HARDLY BELIEVE THEY WERE TO BE SURRENDERED.

TAKE THIS TO GRANT. HE WON'T FORGET THAT I ONCE PAID HIS HOTEL BILL WHEN HE WAS DOWN AND OUT.

BUCKNER SENT A REQUEST FOR TERMS TO GRANT, THINKING HIS OLD PAL WOULD BE AS GENEROUS AS THE CONFEDERATES HAD BEEN AT FORT SUMTER.

THAT UNGENEROUS AND UNCHIVALROUS INGRATE!

no terms but unconditional and immediate surrender.

Grant

BUCKNER RECEIVED GRANT'S REPLY.

JOHNSTON NOW HAD TO ABANDON NASHVILLE. WITH ITS VITAL INDUSTRIES AND POPULATION OF THIRTY THOUSAND, IT WAS THE FIRST IMPORTANT CONFEDERATE CITY TO FALL TO THE INVADERS.

THE FALL OF NASHVILLE WAS CELEBRATED IN THE UNITED STATES. AND GRANT BECAME A NATIONAL HERO.

AS GRANT APPROACHED NASHVILLE FROM THE WEST. AND BUELL FROM THE EAST. JOHNSTON RETREATED TOWARD CHATTANOOGA.

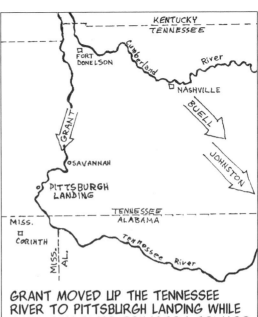

GRANT MOVED UP THE TENNESSEE RIVER TO PITTSBURGH LANDING WHILE BUELL FOLLOWED JOHNSTON TOWARD CHATTANOOGA.

CHAPTER 5

IRON SHIPS
The *Monitor* and the *Virginia*

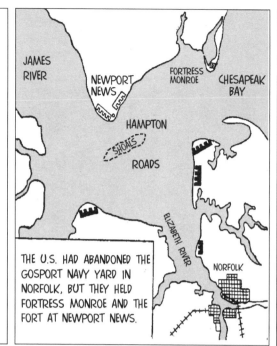

THE U.S. HAD ABANDONED THE GOSPORT NAVY YARD IN NORFOLK, BUT THEY HELD FORTRESS MONROE AND THE FORT AT NEWPORT NEWS.

BEFORE LEAVING, THE YANKEES BURNED ALL THE BUILDINGS AND THE SHIPS THAT COULDN'T BE MOVED TO SAFETY.

IT'S WHAT'S LEFT OF THE U.S.S. *MERRIMACK*, SIR.

SHE SANK TOO FAST TO BURN THE HULL, AND THE ENGINES AND BOILERS LOOK INTACT.

CONFEDERATE LIEUTENANT JOHN BROOKE SAW POTENTIAL IN THE WRECKAGE OF A STEAM FRIGATE.

EVERYTHING ABOVE THE WATER LINE WILL BE COVERED WITH IRON!

I'VE BEEN TRYING TO BUY AN IRONCLAD IN EUROPE WITH NO LUCK. GO AHEAD!

LIEUTENANT BROOKE TOOK HIS IDEA TO THE SECRETARY OF THE NAVY, STEPHEN R. MALLORY.

TWO FEET OF OAK AND PINE COVERED BY FOUR INCHES OF IRON!

THE SOUTHERNERS RAISED THE *MERRIMACK* AND BEGAN THE CONVERSION.

WHEN WORD REACHED THE U.S. NAVY DEPARTMENT THAT THE SOUTH WAS BUILDING AN IRONCLAD, NAVY SECRETARY GIDEON WELLES WENT INTO ACTION.

SWEDISH-BORN INVENTOR JOHN ERICSSON SUBMITTED HIS DESIGN.

SOME IN THE NAVY DEPARTMENT THOUGHT ERICSSON'S DESIGN A JOKE.

NEVERTHELESS, WHEN ERICSSON PROMISED DELIVERY IN *100* DAYS, HE GOT THE CONTRACT.

MARCH 8, 1862

RECHRISTENED AS THE C.S.S. *VIRGINIA*, THE *MERRIMACK* LEFT NORFOLK FOR A TRIAL RUN.

COMMODORE FRANKLIN BUCHANAN, CSN

THE C.S.S. *VIRGINIA* WAS COMMANDED BY FRANKLIN BUCHANAN, FORMERLY SUPERINTENDENT OF THE U.S. NAVAL ACADEMY.

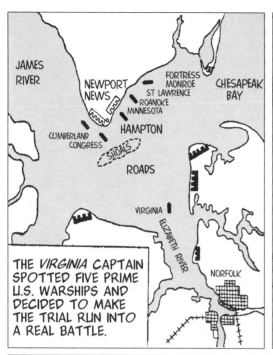

THE *VIRGINIA* CAPTAIN SPOTTED FIVE PRIME U.S. WARSHIPS AND DECIDED TO MAKE THE TRIAL RUN INTO A REAL BATTLE.

THE *VIRGINIA* DROVE HER IRON BEAK THROUGH THE HULL OF THE CUMBERLAND, SINKING HER.

NEXT THE *VIRGINIA* POUNDED THE *CONGRESS* UNTIL THE YANKEE SHIP SURRENDERED.

WHILE THE *VIRGINIA* WAS TAKING ON PRISONERS THE YANKEE COSTAL BATTERIES OPENED FIRE, WOUNDING U.S. AND C.S. CREWMEN ALIKE AND KILLING TWO CONFEDERATE OFFICERS. BUCHANAN WAS ONE OF THE WOUNDED.

THE *VIRGINIA* USED HOT SHOT TO SET FIRES ALL OVER THE *CONGRESS*. UNKNOWN TO BUCHANAN, HIS OWN BROTHER, A U.S.N. LIEUTENANT, DIED IN THE FLAMES.

6:30 A.M., MARCH 9, 1862
LINCOLN'S CABINET MEETS TO DISCUSS THE SITUATION. WAR SECRETARY STANTON PANICS.

LAST NIGHT OUR OWN IRON SHIP REACHED HAMPTON ROADS. SHE SHOULD BE ENGAGING THE *MERRIMACK* AS WE SPEAK.

NAVY SECRETARY WELLES REASSURED THE CABINET.

WHAT?! THAT CHEESE BOX ON A RAFT IS GOING TO SAVE US?

IT ONLY HAS TWO GUNS!

ERICSSON'S INVENTION, CHRISTENED THE U.S.S. *MONITOR*, HAD INDEED ARRIVED AT HAMPTON ROADS. BUT IT LOOKED TOO SMALL TO DEFEAT THE *VIRGINIA*.

ALL THREE RAN AGROUND YESTERDAY. WE'LL PICK THEM OFF ONE BY ONE.

THE *VIRGINIA*, NOW COMMANDED BY LIEUTENANT CATESBY JONES, ENTERED HAMPTON ROADS EXPECTING TO DESTROY THE REMAINING YANKEE WARSHIPS.

AS THE *VIRGINIA* APPROACHED THE *MINNESOTA*, THE *MONITOR* MOVED IN BETWEEN.

PILOT HOUSE

THE IRON SHIPS PUMMELED EACH OTHER FOR HOURS, NEITHER ABLE TO BADLY DAMAGE THE OTHER.

MY EYES! I'M BLIND!

BAM!

JUST AS THE EBBING TIDE FORCED THE *VIRGINIA* TO WITHDRAW TO NORFOLK SHE MADE A DIRECT HIT ON THE SIGHT-SLIT OF THE *MONITOR'S* PILOT HOUSE, TEMPORARILY BLINDING CAPTAIN JOHN WORDEN.

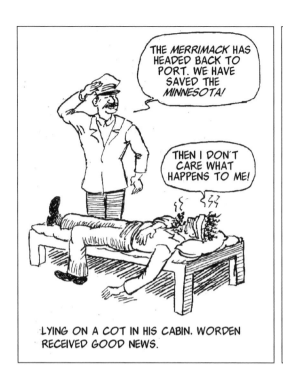

LYING ON A COT IN HIS CABIN. WORDEN RECEIVED GOOD NEWS.

WHO WON THE BATTLE OF THE IRON SHIPS?

IT WAS A DRAW BETWEEN THE TWO VESSELS, BUT IT WAS A DEFEAT FOR THE SOUTH IN THAT THE BLOCKADE WAS NOT BROKEN.

THE BATTLE SIGNALED THE END OF THE ROMANTIC AGE OF TALL WOODEN WARSHIPS. THE FUTURE WAS IRON AND STEAM.

CHAPTER 6

THE PENINSULA

Richmond is so Near
and
Yet so Far

GENERAL GEORGE B. McCLELLAN

WHILE GRANT WAS MAKING HIS REPUTAION IN THE WEST, McCLELLAN WAS STILL BUILDING HIS ARMY OF THE POTOMAC.

IF YOU'RE NOT PLANNING TO USE THIS ARMY, I'D LIKE TO **BORROW** IT.

HEE, HEE. VERY AMUSING MISTER PRESIDENT.

TO NO AVAIL, LINCOLN TRIED HINTING TO McCLELLAN TO GET HIS ARMY INTO ACTION.

GO TAKE RICHMOND OR I'LL FIND A GENERAL WHO WILL!

WHY DIDN'T YOU SAY SO BEFORE?

FINALLY LINCOLN RESORTED TO A MORE DIRECT APPROACH.

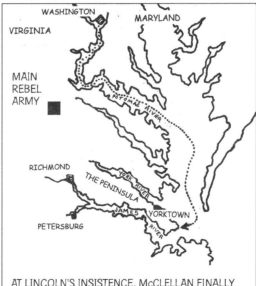

AT LINCOLN'S INSISTENCE, McCLELLAN FINALLY BEGAN HIS "PENINSULA CAMPAIGN." HIS PLAN WAS TO BYPASS THE CONFEDERATE ARMY AND USE THE RIVERS FOR SUPPLYING HIS ARMY.

GENERAL JOSEPH E. JOHNSTON

OPPOSING McCLELLAN WAS ONE OF THE SOUTH'S BEST GENERALS, BUT JOHNSTON COULDN'T MARCH HIS ARMY INTO THE PENINSULA IN TIME TO STOP THE YANKEES.

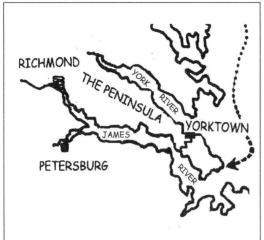

ALL THAT STOOD BETWEEN McCLELLAN'S 100,000 MEN AND RICHMOND WERE 15,000 CONFEDERATES MANNING FORTIFICATIONS STRETCHING FROM YORKTOWN ACROSS THE PENINSULA.

GENERAL JOHN B. MAGRUDER, CSA

THE GENERAL IN CHARGE AT YORKTOWN WAS "PRINCE JOHN" MAGRUDER. HIS JOB WAS TO DELAY THE YANKS UNTIL GEN. JOHNSTON COULD MARCH HIS MAIN ARMY INTO THE PENINSULA.

THESE LOG GUNS SET AMONG THE REAL ONES WILL FOOL THE YANKEES.

MAGRUDER WAS AN AMATEUR THEATRICAL PRODUCER. HE USED HIS STAGE TALENTS TO PERFORM THE GREATEST BLUFF OF THE WAR.

WHOA, NELLIE! THIS IS GONNA BE A TOUGH NUT TO CRACK.

WHEN THE FEDERALS ARRIVED THEY SAW A TREMENDOUS NUMBER OF CANNONS, AND REINFORCEMENTS ARRIVING HOURLY.

FALL IN FOR SIX MORE LAPS.

WILL I SLEEP TONIGHT!

THE "REINFORCEMENTS" WERE THE SAME TROOPS MARCHED ALL DAY IN A CIRCLE.

TAKE ME UP FOR A LOOK-SEE.

YES, SIR, BUT IT'S SORT OF WINDY.

MAGRUDER'S THEATRICS COMPLETELY DECEIVED McCLELLAN, BUT FITZ JOHN PORTER WAS ONE GENERAL WHO WANTED TO SEE FOR HIMSELF WHAT WAS GOING ON IN YORKTOWN.

A SUDDEN GUST OF WIND BREAKS THE TETHER.

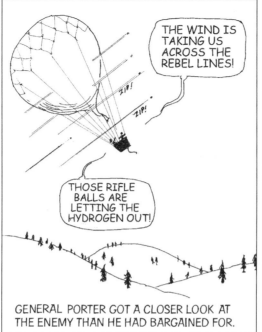

GENERAL PORTER GOT A CLOSER LOOK AT THE ENEMY THAN HE HAD BARGAINED FOR.

FOR AWHILE IT LOOKED AS IF THEY WOULD BE KILLED OR CAPTURED.

GEN. PORTER HAD BEEN TOO BUSY DODGING BULLETS TO SEE MUCH. McCLELLAN ISSUED AN ORDER FORBIDDING GENERAL OFFICERS FROM ASCENDING IN OBSERVATION BALLOONS.

WHILE McCLELLAN WAS WAITING FOR HIS SIEGE GUNS, GENERAL JOHNSTON ARRIVED WITH THE MAIN CONFEDERATE ARMY. HE DECIDED TO PULL OUT OF YORKTOWN AND GIVE BATTLE CLOSER TO RICHMOND.

SOUTHERN INGENUITY

MARCHING IN PURSUIT OF JOHNSTON ALONG THE ROAD TO RICHMOND, THE YANKS ENCOUNTERED A NEW WEAPON NOT SEEN BEFORE IN WARFARE: THE LAND MINE.

47

YANKEE INGENUITY
GENERAL McCLELLAN INVENTS THE FIRST MINE DETECTOR, A ROW OF CONFEDERATE PRISONERS OF WAR FORCED TO WALK AHEAD OF THE UNION TROOPS.

JOHNSTON NOW TOOK THE INITIATIVE AND ATTACKED THE INVADERS AT SEVEN PINES, WHERE HE WAS SEVERELY WOUNDED.

GENERAL ROBERT E. LEE

PRESIDENT DAVIS APPOINTED AN EVEN MORE BRILLIANT COMMANDER TO REPLACE HIM.

McCLELLAN BROUGHT HIS ARMY ALMOST TO THE GATES OF RICHMOND.

THE WHOLE CIVILIAN POPULATION OF RICHMOND TURNED OUT TO HELP THE CONFEDERATE ARMY BUILD DEFENSES.

THE GOVERNMENT WAS PREPARED TO FLEE THE CITY AT A MOMENT'S NOTICE.

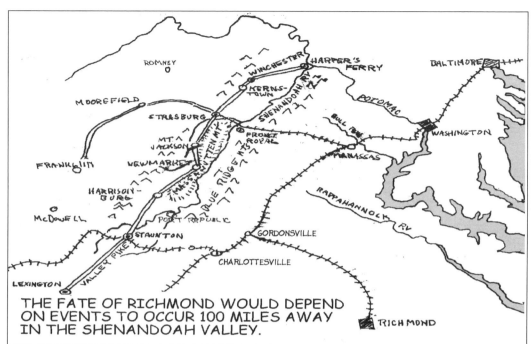

THE FATE OF RICHMOND WOULD DEPEND ON EVENTS TO OCCUR 100 MILES AWAY IN THE SHENANDOAH VALLEY.

THOMAS "STONEWALL" JACKSON'S BRIGADE HAD PERFORMED SO WELL AT MANASSAS THAT HE HAD BEEN GIVEN SEVERAL ADDITIONAL BRIGADES AND PROMOTED TO MAJOR GENERAL. HE HAD THEN BEEN SENT WITH HIS NEW DIVISION TO THE SHENANDOAH VALLEY.

JANUARY 1, 1862

ON A WARM, SUNNY DAY, JACKSON BEGINS A CAMPAIGN TO DRIVE THE FEDERALS OUT OF ROMNEY.

A SUDDEN SNOW STORM PREVENTED THE SUPPLY WAGONS FROM CATCHING UP WITH JACKSON'S ADVANCE.

THE NEXT MORNING THE COLD, STIFF SOLDIERS BRUSHED THE SNOW OFF AND AROSE TO FIND THAT JACKSON HAD COME UP DURING THE NIGHT AND HAD LAIN DOWN AMONG THEM.

BY SHARING THEIR HARDSHIPS JACKSON EARNED THE RESPECT OF HIS MEN.

JACKSON HAD MANY DETAILED MAPS OF THE VALLEY PREPARED, SHOWING EVERYTHING OF THE SLIGHTEST MILITARY SIGNIFICANCE.

BELLE BOYD

JACKSON ALSO CULTIVATED A NETWORK OF INFORMERS AND SPIES. AMONG THE MOST USEFUL WAS AN ATTRACTIVE WASHINGTON DEBUTANTE WHO HAD MOVED BACK TO THE VALLEY WHEN THE WAR STARTED.

BELLE WAS SO CHARMING THAT UNION OFFICERS FORGAVE HER FOR KILLING A SOLDIER WHO HAD FORCED HIS WAY INTO THE BOYD HOME IN MARTINSBURG.

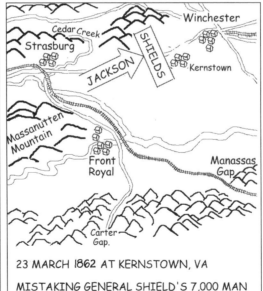

23 MARCH 1862 AT KERNSTOWN, VA

MISTAKING GENERAL SHIELD'S 7,000 MAN DIVISION FOR A MUCH SMALLER FORCE, JACKSON ATTACKS WITH ONLY 3,000 MEN.

JACKSON'S MEN WERE BEATEN BACK, GIVING HIM HIS FIRST (AND LAST) DEFEAT.

McCLELLAN WANTS THE WHOLE ARMY IN THE PENINSULA, BUT I MUST KEEP A STRONG FORCE IN THE VALLEY!

BUT JACKSON'S DEFEAT AT KERNSTOWN HAD THE EFFECT OF A VICTORY BECAUSE IT TIED DOWN UNION FORCES.

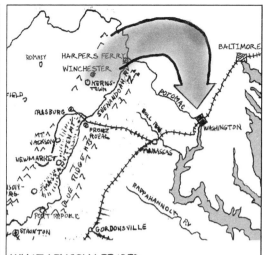

WHAT LINCOLN FEARED

LINCOLN WAS ALWAYS CONCERNED THAT A LARGE CONFEDERATE FORCE MIGHT BE LAUNCHED FROM THE VALLEY TO ATTACK WASHINGTON FROM THE NORTH.

IT WILL BE UP TO GENERAL JACKSON TO KEEP THESE FORCES AWAY FROM THE CAPITOL.

MAY 1862

NOW LEE WOULD USE JACKSON AGAIN TO KEEP McCLELLAN FROM ENLARGING HIS ARMY NEAR RICHMOND.

GENERAL RICHARD S. EWELL, CSA

LEE DEPLETED HIS ALREADY OUTNUMBERED ARMY BY SENDING EWELL'S DIVISION TO SERVE UNDER JACKSON IN HIS CAMPAIGN IN THE SHENANDOAH VALLEY.

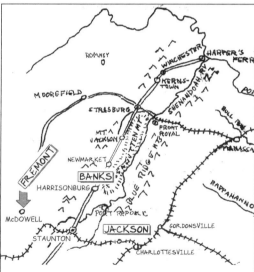

JACKSON'S FIRST CONCERN WAS TO STOP FREMONT FROM SWEEPING THROUGH STAUNTON AND COMBINING HIS FORCE WITH BANKS'S.

WE SHOULDN'T LEAVE WITHOUT FIGHTING THE YANKEES AGAIN.

YOU'RE RIGHT!

JACKSON PRETENDED TO ABANDON THE VALLEY BY MARCHING HIS ARMY TOWARD RICHMOND. EVEN HIS SOLDIERS WERE FOOLED.

AFTER A THREE-DAY MARCH, THEY REACHED THE RAILROAD AND WERE PUT ON A TRAIN. THEY EXPECTED THE TRAIN WOULD MOVE EASTWARD, OUT OF THE VALLEY AND TOWARD RICHMOND.

WHEN THE TRAIN STARTED WESTWARD, THE SOLDIERS CHEERED. THEY WANTED A VICTORY IN THE SHENANDOAH VALLEY BEFORE LEAVING.

LEAVING EWELL'S DIVISION TO WATCH BANKS, JACKSON MOVED THE REST OF HIS ARMY IN A LOOP BACK INTO AND ACROSS THE VALLEY TO ATTACK FREMONT AT McDOWELL, VIRGINIA.

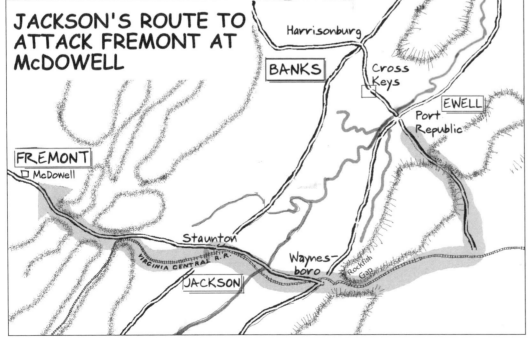

JACKSON'S ROUTE TO ATTACK FREMONT AT McDOWELL

8 MAY 1862

FREMONT'S FORCES ARE DEFEATED, BUT MAKE THEIR ESCAPE BY SETTING FOREST FIRES AS THEY RETREAT.

BANKS HAS MOVED TO STRASBURG, GENERAL JACKSON!

WELL, GENERAL EWELL, LET'S GO GET HIM.

EWELL LEFT HIS DIVISION TO BRING JACKSON THE NEWS THAT BANKS' BEST DIVISION HAD BEEN SENT OUT OF THE THE VALLEY, LEAVING BANKS VULNERABLE.

SEND ONE BRIGADE OF YOUR COMMAND TO ME ON THE TURNPIKE. TAKE THE OTHER TWO BRIGADES DOWN THE SOUTH FORK TO LURAY.

EWELL RECEIVED HIS ORDERS.

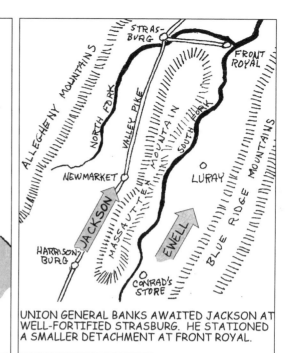

UNION GENERAL BANKS AWAITED JACKSON AT WELL-FORTIFIED STRASBURG. HE STATIONED A SMALLER DETACHMENT AT FRONT ROYAL.

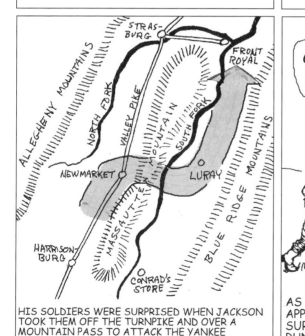

HIS SOLDIERS WERE SURPRISED WHEN JACKSON TOOK THEM OFF THE TURNPIKE AND OVER A MOUNTAIN PASS TO ATTACK THE YANKEE DETACHMENT AT FRONT ROYAL.

GOOD GRIEF!! IT'S A GIRL!

AS THE ADVANCE OF JACKSON'S ARMY APPROACHED FRONT ROYAL, THEY WERE SURPRISED TO SEE A YOUNG WOMAN RUN TO THEM FROM THE WOODS.

...AND HURRY! THEY'RE SETTING FIRE TO THE WAGON BRIDGE - BUT NOT THE RAILROAD BRIDGE.

IT WAS BELLE BOYD. SHE BROUGHT JACKSON VALUABLE INFORMATION ABOUT THE UNION DEFENSES.

GENERAL RICHARD TAYLOR, CSA

BRIGADIER GENERAL RICHARD TAYLOR, THE SON OF U.S. PRESIDENT TAYLOR. HIS BRIGADE WAS THE FIRST TO REACH THE RIVER.

THERE'S NO FLOORING, JUST THE TIES.

HURRY!! THEY'RE SHOOTING AT US!

TAYLOR SENT ONE OF HIS REGIMENTS ACROSS THE RAILROAD BRIDGE UNDER FIRE, STEPPING ON THE CROSS-TIES.

GENERAL TAYLOR LED THE CHARGE ACROSS THE WAGON BRIDGE, WHICH WAS ALREADY ON FIRE. THE YANKEES FLED AS THE SCORCHED REBELS GAINED THE WEST BANK.

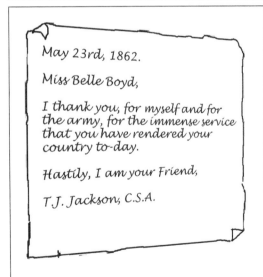

May 23rd, 1862.

Miss Belle Boyd,

I thank you, for myself and for the army, for the immense service that you have rendered your country to-day.

Hastily, I am your Friend,

T.J. Jackson, C.S.A.

JACKSON TOOK TIME FROM PURSUING THE RETREATING YANKS TO WRITE A NOTE THAT WOULD BE CHERISHED FOR THE REST OF A YOUNG LADY'S LIFE.

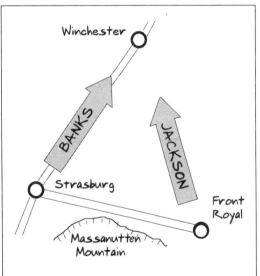

Winchester

BANKS

JACKSON

Strasburg

Front Royal

Massanutten Mountain

WHEN UNION GENERAL BANKS LEARNED THAT FRONT ROYAL HAD FALLEN, HE WITHDREW FROM STRASBURG TOWARD MARYLAND. JACKSON CAUGHT UP WITH HIM AT WINCHESTER.

WHAT THE ♒♓☀♎♏♏❖ ARE YOU DODGING FOR?

DURING THE FIGHTING AT WINCHESTER, GENERAL TAYLOR FORGOT THE PRESENCE OF JACKSON AND YELLED PROFANITIES AT HIS MEN.

HE WAS EMBARRASSED WHEN JACKSON GENTLY ADMONISHED HIM.

BUT WHEN TAYLOR LED HIS MEN TO VICTORY, JACKSON WAS THERE TO EXTEND HIS HAND IN A SILENT BUT MEANINGFUL TRIBUTE.

BANKS WAS DRIVEN COMPLETELY OUT OF VIRGINIA INTO MARYLAND ACROSS THE POTOMAC RIVER.

3,000 PRISONERS, 10,000 SMALL ARMS, 6 CANNONS, TONS OF BLANKETS AND CLOTHING, AND VAST QUANTITIES OF MEDICAL STORES - IT WAS VITAL TO KEEP THESE FROM BEING RECAPTURED.

LINCOLN SAW A CHANCE TO TRAP JACKSON. HE ORDERED FREMONT, BANKS, AND SHIELDS TO ATTACK FROM THREE SIDES AT THE SAME TIME.

EWELL'S DIVISION HELD FREMONT OFF UNTIL JACKSON'S FARTHEST REGIMENTS HAD PASSED STRASBURG AND FOLLOWED THE WAGON TRAIN SOUTHWARD, UP THE VALLEY.

BANKS HAD LOST SO MUCH OF HIS SUPPLIES TO JACKSON THAT HE ADVANCED NO FARTHER THAN WINCHESTER.

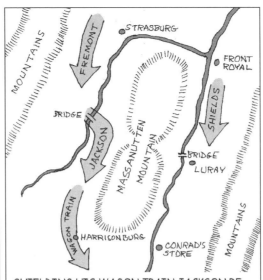

SHIELDING HIS WAGON TRAIN JACKSON RETREATED BEFORE FREMONT WHILE SHIELDS MOVED UP THE OTHER SIDE OF MASSANUTTEN. IF THE UNION FORCES COULD COMBINE THEY WOULD BE TOO POWEFUL FOR JACKSON.

TO KEEP THE FEDERAL FORCES FROM UNITING, JACKSON'S CAVALRY BURNED BRIDGES ON BOTH FORKS OF THE SHENANDOAH RIVER.

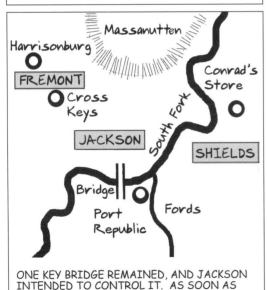

ONE KEY BRIDGE REMAINED, AND JACKSON INTENDED TO CONTROL IT. AS SOON AS HIS WAGON TRAIN WAS SAFELY SOUTH OF PORT REPUBLIC, JACKSON WOULD ATTACK FIRST ONE UNION FORCE AND THEN THE OTHER.

WHILE JACKSON HEADED THE REST OF HIS ARMY EASTWARD TO MEET SHIELDS, EWELL'S DIVISION MET FREMONT AT CROSS KEYS.

EWELL LEFT A SMALL BLUFFING FORCE FACING FREMONT AT CROSS KEYS, AND HURRIED TO PORT REPUBLIC.

JACKSON SENT TAYLOR'S BRIGADE TO SEIZE THE WELL-PLACED UNION ARTILLERY THAT HAD STOPPED THE CONFEDERATE ADVANCE.

QUICK, BEFORE THEY GET AWAY!

TAYLOR'S MEN TOOK THE CANNONS TWICE BUT WERE DRIVEN OFF. ON THE THIRD ATTEMPT THEY HELD THE GUNS AND TRAINED THEM ON THE ENEMY.

JACKSON THEN ORDERED A GENERAL ADVANCE THAT DROVE THE YANKEES BACK FOUR MILES.

SHIELDS AND FREMONT STILL CAN'T JOIN FORCES UNTIL THEY REBUILD THAT BRIDGE.

THE VICTORIOUS REBELS REGROUPED AT PORT REPUBLIC AND JACKSON LED HIS ARMY TOWARD RICHMOND TO REINFORCE LEE.

WE'VE CAPTURED THOUSANDS OF PRISONERS, DOZENS OF CANNONS, TONS OF BLANKETS AND CLOTHING, AND A WHOLE WAREHOUSE OF MEDICAL SUPPLIES.

HE WHO DOES NOT SEE THE HAND OF GOD IN THIS IS BLIND, SIR, BLIND!

JACKSON AND EWELL WERE WELL PLEASED WITH THEIR CAMPAIGN. JACKSON'S CORPS OF 18,000 HAD KEPT 40,000 YANKS AWAY FROM RICHMOND.

JACKSON'S ACTIVITIES IN THE VALLEY KEPT McCLELLAN FROM RECEIVING THE REINFORCEMENTS THAT WOULD HAVE ASSURED THE FALL OF RICHMOND.

WELL BEFORE LINCOLN THOUGHT THE VALLEY WAS SAFE ENOUGH TO LEAVE UNGUARDED, JACKSON ARRIVED IN THE PENINSULA TO ASSIST LEE.

THE SEVEN DAYS

DESPITE BEING GREATLY OUTNUMBERED, LEE TOOK THE OFFENSIVE AND PROVOKED SIX MAJOR BATTLES WITHIN A WEEK'S TIME. ALTHOUGH McCLELLAN RETREATED AFTER EACH BATTLE, MOST WERE UNION VICTORIES IN TERMS OF CASUALTIES. LEE'S AUDACITY CONVINCED McCLELLAN THAT HE WAS OPPOSED BY A MUCH LARGER FORCE.

THE LAST OF THE BATTLES WAS AT MALVERN HILL.

ALTHOUGH McCLELLAN GREATLY OUTNUMBERED LEE, HE THOUGHT IT WAS THE OTHER WAY AROUND AND GAVE UP ON TAKING RICHMOND.

CHAPTER 7

SHILOH
Two Tough Days

AS GRANT APPROACHED NASHVILLE FROM THE WEST, AND BUELL FROM THE EAST, JOHNSTON RETREATED TOWARD CHATTANOOGA.

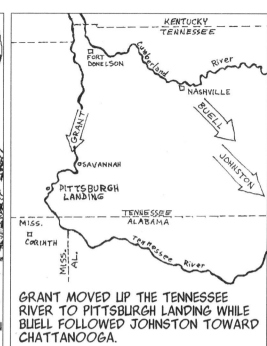

GRANT MOVED UP THE TENNESSEE RIVER TO PITTSBURGH LANDING WHILE BUELL FOLLOWED JOHNSTON TOWARD CHATTANOOGA.

MEANWHILE JOHNSTON WAS HAVING ALL THE FORCES PRESIDENT DAVIS WOULD GIVE HIM SENT TO HIS SECOND-IN-COMMAND, BEAUREGARD, IN CORINTH, MISSISSIPPI.

FINALLY JOHNSTON HIMSELF ARRIVED IN CORINTH WITH THE REST OF HIS ARMY.

JOHNSTON AND BEAUREGARD TALK STRATEGY.

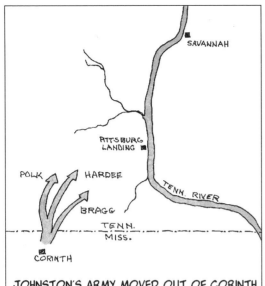

JOHNSTON'S ARMY MOVED OUT OF CORINTH IN THREE COLUMNS LED BY CSA GENERALS POLK. HARDEE AND BRAGG.

GRANT WAS A FEW MILES DOWNRIVER AT SAVANNAH, TENNESSEE.

GEN. WILLIAM TECUMSEH SHERMAN
THE CAMP WAS UNDER THE COMMAND OF GENERAL SHERMAN.

APRIL 6. 1862

THE U.S. TROOPS WERE HAVING BREAKFAST WHEN THE CONFEDERATES STRUCK.

GRANT HEARD THE BATTLE FROM HIS HEADQUARTERS IN SAVANNAH.

HE HURRIED UPSTREAM TOWARD THE BATTLE.

THE UNION MEN FOUGHT WELL. BUT THE CONFEDERATES FORCED THEM BACK TOWARD THE RIVER.

LAND SAKES! OF COURSE NOT.

GENERAL LEONIDAS POLK, CSA
CONFEDERATE CORPS COMMANDER POLK WAS AN EPISCOPAL BISHOP AND NEVER USED PROFANITY.

BOYS, GIVE THOSE !%÷#@*& YANKEES ʒ*@÷¿¿!

ONE OF HIS BRIGADE COMMANDERS, THOUGH, WAS GEN. BENJAMIN CHEATHAM, WHO WAS AN EXPERT AT SWEARING.

AHEMMM!

OOPS!

MEN, YOU HEARD GENERAL CHEATHAM! GIVE THEM **WHAT HE SAID!**

IT'S LIKE BEING IN A **HORNETS NEST** OF BULLETS!

STAY LOW AND KEEP FIRING!

THE CONFEDERATE ADVANCE STALLED WHEN ONE U.S. REGIMENT STUBBORNLY CLUNG TO A SUNKEN ROAD.

JOHNSTON SENT HIS STAFF SURGEON TO TREAT WOUNDED PRISONERS. THIS ACT OF MERCY WOULD COST THE GENERAL HIS LIFE.

JOHNSTON RALLIED HIS TROOPS FOR A FINAL ASSAULT ON THE STUBBORN YANKEES.

INSPIRED BY JOHNSTON, THE CONFEDERATES SUCCEEDED IN DRIVING THE U.S. FORCES FROM THEIR POSITION.

AFTER THE CHARGE JOHNSTON RETURNED TO HIS STAFF ELATED AND APPARENTLY UNHARMED.

BUT AS HE WAS SPEAKING HE COLLAPSED.

HIS STAFF LAID HIM DOWN AND TRIED TO HELP.

A BULLET HAD CUT THE LARGE ARTERY IN HIS LEG, AND WITHIN JUST A FEW MINUTES JOHNSTON BLED TO DEATH.

THE COMMAND OF THE C.S. ARMY PASSED TO BEAUREGARD, BUT HE WAS SICK AND UNABLE TO MOVE TO THE BATTLE FRONT.

WHEN GRANT ARRIVED AT PITTSBURGH LANDING HE FOUND THE BANKS CROWDED WITH SOLDIERS WHO HAD FLED THE BATTLE.

FAILING TO RALLY THE SOLDIERS ON THE BANK, GRANT REFORMED HIS LINE FOR A LAST DITCH DEFENSE OF THE LANDING.

AS DARKNESS APPROACHED, U.S. GUNBOATS ARRIVED AND BEGAN AN INEFFECTUAL SHELLING OF THE CONFEDERATES.

THINKING THAT HIS FORCES WERE BEING POUNDED BY THE GUNBOATS, BEAUREGARD COMMITTED ONE OF THE MAJOR BLUNDERS OF THE WAR.

THE CORPS COMMANDERS WANTED TO CONTINUE THE ADVANCE, BUT OBEYED BEAUREGARD'S ORDERS.

AFTER DARK BUELL ARRIVED. ALL DURING THE NIGHT HIS ARMY WAS FERRIED ACROSS THE TENNESSEE RIVER TO DOUBLE THE SIZE OF THE U.S. FORCE.

COLONEL FORREST SAW THE FERRIES AND VAINLY SEARCHED FOR BEAUREGARD TO WARN HIM.

ENCOURAGED BY THE REINFORCEMENTS, GRANT'S DISPIRITED TROOPS LEFT THE RIVER BANK, TOOK UP THEIR WEAPONS, AND REJOINED THEIR MORE RESOLUTE COMRADES.

AT DAWN THE C.S. FORCES RESUMED THEIR ATTACK BUT SOON FOUND THEMSELVES DRIVEN BACK BY THE GREATLY ENLARGED U.S. ARMY.

FORREST'S REGIMENT PROTECTED THE REAR WHILE THE CONFEDERATES MADE AN ORDERLY RETREAT TOWARD CORINTH.

DURING THE CHARGE FORREST GOT TOO FAR IN FRONT OF HIS MEN AND FOUND HIMSELF SURROUNDED BY THE ENEMY.

ONE SOLDIER FIRED HIS RIFLE POINTBLANK INTO FORREST'S SIDE WHILE ANOTHER CLAMBERED UP TO PULL HIM DOWN.

SEIZING THE SOLDIER IN HIS POWERFUL GRIP, FORREST GALLOPED BACK TO HIS MEN.

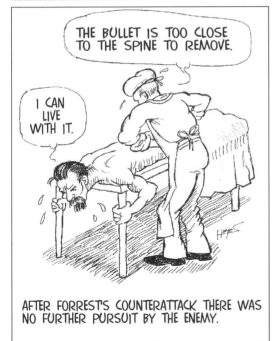

AFTER FORREST'S COUNTERATTACK THERE WAS NO FURTHER PURSUIT BY THE ENEMY.

THE BATTLE OF PITTSBURGH LANDING, SO FAR THE BLOODIEST OF THE WAR, HAD BEEN FOUGHT NEAR A LITTLE COUNTRY CHURCH.

BECAUSE OF THE HIGH NUMBER OF CASUALTIES AND NEAR DEFEAT AT SHILOH, GENERAL HALLECK SIDELINED GRANT AND TOOK PERSONAL COMMAND OF HIS ARMY, WHICH NOW WOULD ACT WITH EXTREME CAUTION UNTIL GRANT WAS RESTORED TO COMMAND FOR THE VICKSBURG CAMPAIGN.

CHAPTER 8

NEW ORLEANS
The South's Greatest Port

ABOUT ONE HUNDRED MILES UP THE MISSISSIPPI LAY THE CONFEDERACY'S LARGEST CITY AND GREATEST PORT, NEW ORLEANS.

NEW ORLEANS

FT. SAINT PHILIP

FORT JACKSON

THE CITY WAS PROTECTED BY TWO FORTS ABOUT NINETY MILES DOWNRIVER.

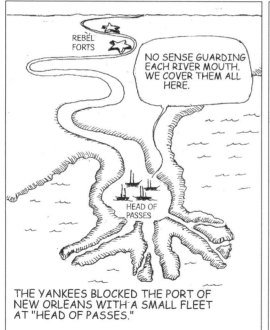

REBEL FORTS

NO SENSE GUARDING EACH RIVER MOUTH. WE COVER THEM ALL HERE.

HEAD OF PASSES

THE YANKEES BLOCKED THE PORT OF NEW ORLEANS WITH A SMALL FLEET AT "HEAD OF PASSES."

I'VE GOT ONLY ONE TRUE WARSHIP, BUT I'LL STICK GUNS ON ANYTHING THAT STEAMS!

CAPTAIN GEORGE N. HOLLINS, IN CHARGE OF THE CONFEDERATE FLEET IN NEW ORLEANS, DECIDED TO ATTACK THE BLOCKADERS.

I'LL RENT IT TO YOU, BUT YOU WON'T LIKE THE PRICE!

I'M SEIZING YOUR VESSEL. THE NAVY WILL EVENTUALLY PAY YOU, BUT YOU WON'T LIKE THE PRICE.

FIXED GUN

IRON PLATES

IRON RAM

128 ft 385 tons

A LOCAL BUSINESSMAN WAS BUILDING AN IRON-CLAD RAM AS A MONEY-MAKING VENTURE HOLLINS COMMANDEERED IT AND NAMED IT THE CSN *MANASSAS*.

OCTOBER 12, 1861, BEFORE DAWN---
A STRANGE SQUADRON ON A DARING
MISSION APPROACHES THE BLOCKADERS.

THE U.S. FLEET HAD NOT POSTED WATCHES
AND DIDN'T SEE THE LOW SILHOUETTE OF
THE *MANASSAS* UNTIL IT WAS UPON THEM.

IN THE PREDAWN DARKNESS THE *MANASSAS*
CHARGES THE U.S. FLAGSHIP *RICHMOND* AT FULL
SPEED AUGMENTED BY A SWIFT RIVER CURRENT.

FIRING ITS CANNONS BLINDLY, THE STRICKEN
RICHMOND RUNS AGROUND. AS REBEL FIRE
RAFTS DRIFT TOWARD THE YANKEE FLEET, THE
BLOCKADERS FLEE FOR THE GULF.

THERE WERE NO SHIPS OR MEN LOST, BUT
IT WAS A GREAT MORAL VICTORY FOR THE
SOUTH, AND U.S. SECRETARY OF NAVY
GIDEON WELLES WAS INFURIATED

COMMANDER DAVID D. PORTER BROUGHT A
PLAN TO SECRETARY WELLES FOR CAPTURING
NEW ORLEANS.

BECAUSE FARRAGUT WAS FROM THE SOUTH, MARRIED TO A SOUTHERNER, AND HIS FATHER WAS A SPANIARD, HIS LOYALTY HAD BEEN QUESTIONED.

"YES, SIR. BEFORE I WAS BORN, FARRAGUT WAS INFORMALLY ADOPTED BY MY FATHER, COMMODORE PORTER, AND WENT TO SEA AT THE AGE OF NINE..."

"...MY FATHER BECAME A GREAT HERO OF THE WAR OF 1812. ABOUT THE TIME I WAS BORN, HE PUT FARRAGUT IN COMMAND OF A CAPTURED SHIP AT THE AGE OF TWELVE..."

"..HE FOUGHT PIRATES IN THE CARRIBEAN AND THE BARBARY COAST, AND DISTINGUISHED HIMSELF IN THE MEXICAN WAR. HE'S OVER SIXTY NOW, BUT KEEPS FIT BY FENCING WITH YOUNGER OFFICERS..."

CAPTAIN DAVID C. FARRAGUT, USN

FARRAGUT WAS DELIGHTED TO RECEIVE COMMAND OF THE NEW ORLEANS INVASION FLEET.

BY MID-APRIL, 1862, THE FLOTILLA OF TWENTY MORTAR SCHOONERS WERE ALL IN PLACE OUT OF SIGHT OF THE FORTS.

PORTER'S PLAN ALLOWED FORTY-EIGHT HOURS TO SILENCE THE FORTS. BUT AFTER FIVE DAYS OF UNCEASING BOMBARDMENT THE FORTS WERE STILL RETURNING FIRE. FARRAGUT DECIDED NOT TO WAIT ANY LONGER.

24 APRIL 1862, 2:00 AM

FARRAGUT STARTS THE INVASION FLEET IN A RUN PAST THE FORTS.

AS THE U.S. FLEET FOUGHT ITS WAY PAST THE FORTS, IT WAS MET BY THE WEAK BUT GAME CONFEDERATE DEFENSE FLEET.

THE LITTLE CONFEDERATE RAM *MANASSAS* DIDN'T HAVE ENOUGH POWER TO BREAK THE WARSHIPS' HULLS.

THE *MANASSAS* CAUGHT FIRE, EXPLODED AND SANK.

THE UNARMED REBEL TUG *MOSHER* PUSHED THE *HARTFORD* AGROUND AND HELD A FIRE RAFT AGAINST IT UNTIL THE WARSHIP SHOT THE LITTLE TUG TO PIECES AND SANK IT.

By that time, the flagship had caught fire. Only Farragut's will and the discipline of the crew saved the ship.

The Confederate fleet was soon destroyed, and Farragut stopped above the forts to bury the Union dead. The cost to the Union: one ship, thirty-seven killed, and one hundred forty-six wounded.

The Confederate States force originally stationed at New Orleans had been sent to the Battle of Shiloh and had not returned. So the city itself was undefended.

Without further resistance, Farragut steamed into New Orleans and took possession of the city.

GENERAL BENJAMIN F. BUTLER, USA
After the U.S. Navy captured New Orleans the army moved in to occupy it. General Butler was in command.

Butler instituted a harsh regime. One of his first actions was to order a civilian hanged for cutting down a U.S. flag.

THE GENERAL'S HABIT OF CONFISCATING SILVERWARE LED THE CITIZENS TO CALL HIM "SPOONS" BUTLER.

MIFFED AT THE DISRESPECT SHOWN BY NEW ORLEANS LADIES TOWARD HIS MEN AND OFFICERS, BUTLER ISSUED HIS INFAMOUS GENERAL ORDERS NUMBER 28.

AFTER THIS, "SPOONS" BUTLER BECAME "BEAST" BUTLER, THE MOST HATED OF ALL YANKEES.

NO SOUTHERNER RESPECTED "BEAST" BUTLER.

CHAPTER 9

LEE VERSUS POPE
Back to Manassas

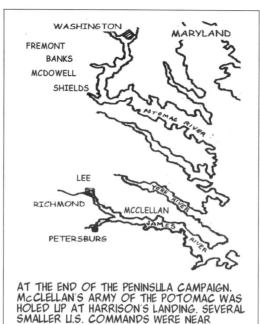

AT THE END OF THE PENINSULA CAMPAIGN, McCLELLAN'S ARMY OF THE POTOMAC WAS HOLED UP AT HARRISON'S LANDING. SEVERAL SMALLER U.S. COMMANDS WERE NEAR WASHINGTON.

REINFORCEMENTS! I WON'T MOVE WITHOUT THEM.

ALTHOUGH McCLELLAN STILL OUTNUMBERED LEE, HE REFUSED TO MOVE FROM HIS BASE AT HARRISON'S LANDING ON THE JAMES.

I NEED A NEW COMMANDER — SOMEONE **AGGRESSIVE**!

LINCOLN DECIDED TO UNITE THE FORCES DEFENDING WASHINGTON INTO A SINGLE ARMY LARGE ENOUGH TO ATTACK RICHMOND.

GEN. JOHN POPE, USA

LINCOLN CHOSE JOHN POPE BECAUSE HE HAD SHOWN INITIATIVE IN THE WESTERN THEATER.

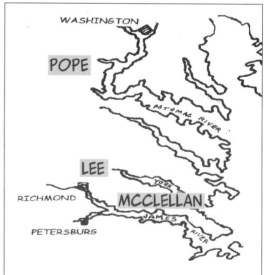

NOW LEE HAD TO CONTEND WITH TWO LARGE U.S. ARMIES IN VIRGINIA.

POPE INTRODUCED HIMSELF TO HIS ARMY BY MAKING A BOASTFUL SPEECH.

HIS MEN TOOK POPE'S SPEECH AS AN INSULT.

LEE'S LITTLE JOKE.

McCLELLAN HAD BEEN CONSIDERATE OF THE SOUTHERN CIVILIANS. POPE CHANGED ALL THAT.

HE ORDERED THAT CAPTURED REBEL GUERRILLAS BE HANGED.

LEE SENT JACKSON TO DEAL WITH POPE.

THAT'S BANKS' CORPS ADVANCING ON US.

GOOD OLD BANKS! HE'S ALWAYS READY FOR A FIGHT! AND HE USUALLY GETS WHIPPED.

AT CEDAR MOUNTAIN JACKSON MET THE ADVANCE OF POPE'S ARMY. A CORPS COMMANDED BY HIS OLD ENEMY FROM THE SHENANDOAH VALLEY, GENERAL BANKS.

FORWARD! WE'LL SHOW THEM WHO'S AFRAID TO FIGHT!

HIS 10,000 MEN WERE OUTNUMBERED, BUT BANKS WAS EAGER TO RESTORE HIS REPUTATION, WHICH HAD SUFFERED IN THE SHENANDOAH VALLEY.

FOLLOW OLD JACK! WE'LL DRIVE THEM BACK!

I NEVER SAW HIM DRAW HIS SWORD BEFORE!

BANKS WAS WINNING UNTIL JACKSON PERSONALLY APPEARED ON THE FIELD TO ENCOURAGE HIS MEN.

GOOD WORK MEN! WE NEARLY WHIPPED THEM!

ALTHOUGH BANKS WAS DEFEATED, HIS AGGRESSIVE ACTION AND NEAR WIN RESTORED HIS REPUTATION AS A FIGHTING GENERAL.

GEN. JAMES LONGSTREET, CSA

McCLELLAN'S ARMY WAS BEING TRANSFERRED PIECEMEAL TO POPE, SO LEE LEFT A SMALL FORCE TO PROTECT RICHMOND AND TOOK LONGSTREET'S CORPS TO JOIN JACKSON.

ANOTHER OF LEE'S GENERALS WAS DASHING J.E.B. STUART, IN CHARGE OF MOST OF THE CAVALRY.

STUART WAS SURPRISED ONE NIGHT WHILE RESTING ON A PORCH.

STUART ESCAPED IN A HAIL OF BULLETS.

POPE KEPT STUART'S FAMOUS PLUMED HAT AND SCARLET CLOAK AS WAR TROPHIES.

LATER, AS STUART LED A NIGHT RAID ON A RAILROAD BEHIND POPE'S LINES, A SUDDEN, HEAVY RAINSTORM OCCURED.

STUART KNEW ONE OF THE PRISONERS. HE AGREED TO LEAD THEM TO POPE'S TENT.

POPE WASN'T IN HIS TENT, BUT A PAYROLL OF $35,000 WAS, AND SO WAS HIS DRESS UNIFORM.

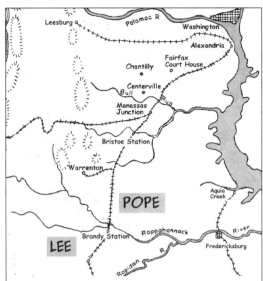

LEE WANTED TO LURE POPE AWAY FROM THE REINFORCEMENTS BUILDING UP AT AQUIA CREEK AS McCLELLAN'S ARMY WAS RECALLED.

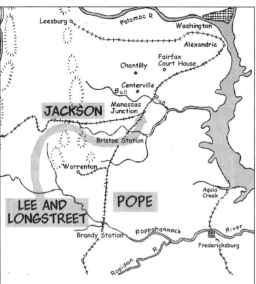

TO DO THIS HE DIVIDED HIS FORCES, SENDING JACKSON AROUND TO POPE'S REAR WHILE KEEPING LONGSTREET IN HIS FRONT.

THERE'S A SQUARE MILE OF WAREHOUSES, SIR, AND HUNDREDS OF LOADED BOXCARS!

LET OUR BOYS TAKE WHAT THEY WANT AND BURN THE REST.

WHAT IS THIS STUFF? IT TASTES AWFUL!

POUR IT OUT. IT'S NOT FIT TO DRINK!

AMONG THE PRIZES WERE BARRELS OF A STRANGE DRINK INTENDED FOR A U.S. DIVISION OF GERMAN IMMIGRANTS. IT WAS THE FIRST TIME THE SOUTHERNERS HAD ENCOUNTERED BEER, AND THEY DIDN'T LIKE IT.

NEW SHOES AND TROUSERS FOR ME!

CHAMPAGNE, CAVIAR, CANNED OYSTERS... WHERE'S THE GRITS?

THE CONFEDERATE TROOPS HAD NEVER SEEN SUCH BOUNTY.

I'M TOTING ABOUT TWO WEEKS OF RATIONS!

I HOPE NOBODY SHOOTS ME FOR A YANKEE!

STUFFED WITH FOOD AND WEARING NEW CLOTHES, THE CONFEDERATES SET FIRE TO THE REMAINING SUPPLIES AND LEFT.

POPE SAW JACKSON'S RAID ON HIS SUPPLIES AS AN OPPORTUNITY.

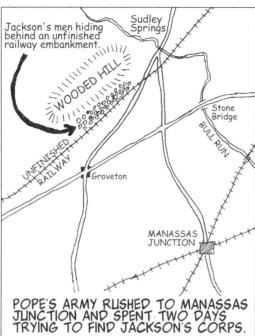

POPE'S ARMY RUSHED TO MANASSAS JUNCTION AND SPENT TWO DAYS TRYING TO FIND JACKSON'S CORPS.

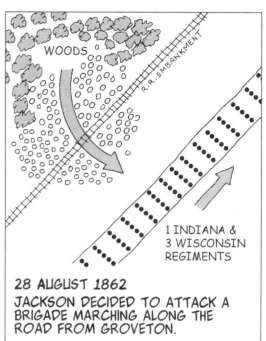

28 AUGUST 1862
JACKSON DECIDED TO ATTACK A BRIGADE MARCHING ALONG THE ROAD FROM GROVETON.

THE US UNIT JACKSON DECIDED TO ATTACK WAS CALLED THE "BLACK HAT" BRIGADE BECAUSE OF THE DISTINCTIVE HEADWEAR SUPPLIED BY THEIR COMMANDER.

THE BRIGADE HAD NEVER BEEN IN COMBAT BEFORE AND SHOULD HAVE BEEN EASY VICTIMS FOR JACKSON'S VETERANS.

BUT THE BRIGADE STOOD AND FOUGHT LIKE VETERANS. LOSING A THIRD OF THEIR NUMBER BEFORE FALLING BACK IN GOOD ORDER.

AMONG THOSE STRUCK DOWN BY THE BLACK HATS WAS JACKSON'S MOST TRUSTED SUBORDINATE, GENERAL RICHARD EWELL.

HAVING REVEALED HIS LOCATION, JACKSON TOOK A STRONG DEFENSIVE POSITION AND AWAITED POPE'S ATTACK.

WHEN POPE GATHERED HIS MAIN ARMY AND FOUND JACKSON STILL ISOLATED, HE WAS OVERJOYED.

AUGUST 20, 1862

ALL DAY JACKSON BEAT BACK REPEATED ATTACKS FROM POPE. MEANWHILE, UNOBSERVED BY POPE, LONGSTREET ARRIVED AND TOOK HIS POSITION ON JACKSON'S RIGHT FLANK.

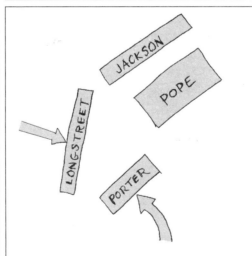

FITZ JOHN PORTER WAS THE FIRST GENERAL TO ARRIVE FROM McCLELLAN'S ARMY. HE WARNED POPE THAT LONGSTREET WAS PRESENT AND TOOK UP A POSITION TO PROTECT POPE'S LEFT FLANK.

POPE DIDN'T TRUST PORTER BECAUSE HE WAS ONE OF McCLELLAN'S FAVORITES.

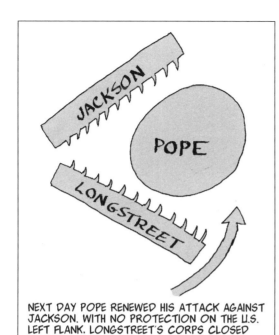

NEXT DAY POPE RENEWED HIS ATTACK AGAINST JACKSON. WITH NO PROTECTION ON THE U.S. LEFT FLANK. LONGSTREET'S CORPS CLOSED LIKE A LOWER JAW ON POPE'S ARMY.

THOUGH MORE ORDERLY THAN THE ROUT A YEAR AGO AT FIRST MANASSAS. THE UNION DEFEAT WAS COMPLETE.

ON HIS RETREAT TOWARD WASHINGTON POPE MET A FAMILIAR FIGURE. LINCOLN HAD SENT McCLELLAN TO TAKE CHARGE.

LINCOLN SENT POPE TO MINNESOTA WHERE HE SPENT THE REST OF THE WAR FIGHTING INDIANS.

CHAPTER 10

SHARPSBURG
Rematch: Lee vs. McClellan

AFTER SECOND MANASSAS LEE TOOK HIS ARMY INTO MARYLAND.

THEY WERE A YEAR LATE. THEIR HAGGARD APPEARANCE DISCOURAGED MARYLANDERS FROM JOINING THEM.

AT FREDERICK THE RECEPTION WAS MIXED.

NEVERTHELESS, THE CAVALRY'S BALL WAS WELL ATTENDED.

AND GOD BLESS OUR PRESIDENT, ABE LINCOLN!

AS WAS HIS CUSTOM, JACKSON ATTENDED A LOCAL CHURCH. THE MINISTER MADE A BOLD PRAYER IN DEFIANCE OF HIS FAMOUS GUEST.

ZZZZZZZ

JACKSON DIDN'T HEAR THE PRAYER BECAUSE IT WAS ALSO HIS CUSTOM TO SLEEP SOUNDLY THROUGH THE SERVICE.

THEY EXPECT US TO ATTACK BALTIMORE. SO WE'LL SURPRISE THEM BY TAKING HARRISBURG, AN IMPORTANT RAIL CENTER.

CAMPED OUTSIDE FREDERICK, LEE ADVISED LONGSTREET AND JACKSON ON HIS STRATEGY FOR THE CAMPAIGN.

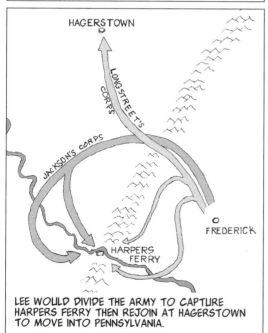

HAGERSTOWN

LONGSTREET'S CORPS

JACKSON'S CORPS

FREDERICK

HARPERS FERRY

LEE WOULD DIVIDE THE ARMY TO CAPTURE HARPERS FERRY THEN REJOIN AT HAGERSTOWN TO MOVE INTO PENNSYLVANIA.

IF McCLELLAN ACTS FAST HE CAN HIT US WHILE THE ARMY IS DIVIDED!

McCLELLAN NEVER ACTS FAST!

LEE'S PLAN WAS BASED ON HIS KNOWLEDGE OF McCLELLAN'S CAUTIOUS NATURE.

LET'S SEE. ONE FOR LONGSTREET AND ONE FOR JACKSON...

AND D.H. HILL AND A.P. HILL AND WALKER AND HOOD AND...

SPECIAL ORDER NO. 191
LEE WROTE OUT THE CAMPAIGN PLAN IN DETAIL, AND THE STAFF OFFICERS MADE COPIES FOR ALL THE DIVISION COMMANDERS.

81

THERE'S ONE LEFT OVER. I'LL USE IT TO WRAP MY CIGARS!

AN EXTRA COPY WAS ACCIDENTALLY MADE. INSTEAD OF DESTROYING IT, AN UNKNOWN STAFF OFFICER USED IT CASUALLY.

TIME TO MOUNT AND RIDE.

THEN HE CARELESSLY LOST HIS CIGAR PACKAGE.

AH, CIGARS! BUT WHAT'S THIS WRAPPER?

HOLY SMOKE! IT'S AN ORDER FROM GEN. LEE!

LATER, WHEN THE U.S. ARMY MOVED INTO THE ABANDONED CONFEDERATE CAMPSITE A YANKEE CORPORAL FOUND THE PACKAGE.

IF I CAN'T WHIP BOBBY LEE WITH THIS I'LL BE WILLING TO GO HOME!

WHEN LEE'S LOST ORDER WAS BROUGHT TO McCLELLAN HE WAS ELATED.

GENERAL D. H. HILL, CSA

AFTER CROSSING THE MOUNTAINS LEE DIVIDED HIS ARMY AS PLANNED, LEAVING ONLY ONE DIVISION UNDER HARVEY HILL TO GUARD THE PASSES.

GET THIS MESSAGE TO GENERAL LEE, PRONTO!

HILL SENT ALARMING NEWS TO LEE: McCLELLAN WAS RUSHING HIS ENTIRE ARMY TOWARD THE MOUNTAIN PASSES.

THE BATTLE OF
SOUTH MOUNTAIN

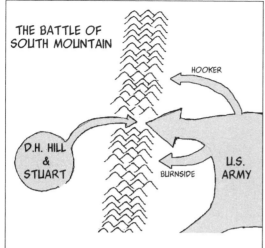

SUNDAY, SEPTEMBER 14, 1862

LEE ORDERED LONGSTREET BACK FROM HAGERSTOWN, BUT ONLY STUART'S CAVALRY WAS ON HAND TO HELP HARVEY HILL HOLD TURNER'S GAP.

IT'S SUNDOWN! WE'VE HELD 'EM OFF ALL DAY.

AFTER DARK WE'LL SLIP AWAY TO JOIN LONGSTREET!

UNDER HARVEY HILL'S LEADERSHIP TWO CS DIVISIONS HELD THE PASS AGAINST TWO US CORPS UNTIL LONGSTREET ARRIVED.

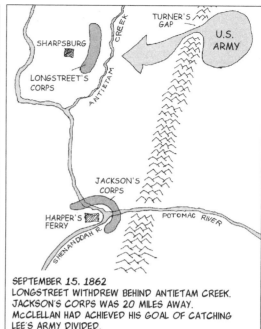

SEPTEMBER 15, 1862
LONGSTREET WITHDREW BEHIND ANTIETAM CREEK. JACKSON'S CORPS WAS 20 MILES AWAY. McCLELLAN HAD ACHIEVED HIS GOAL OF CATCHING LEE'S ARMY DIVIDED.

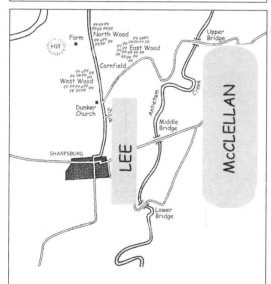

DESPITE OUTNUMBERING LEE 3 TO 1, McCLELLAN DID NOT ATTACK FOR TWO DAYS. THIS GAVE JACKSON TIME TO COMPLETE HIS CAPTURE OF HARPERS FERRY AND REJOIN LEE.

WE'VE CAPTURED 11,000 MEN, 73 CANNONS, 200 WAGONS, AND 13,000 RIFLES AND PISTOLS.

I'LL LEAVE POWELL HILL TO WRAP THINGS UP, AND WE'LL HURRY TO SHARPSBURG.

SEPTEMBER 15, 1862
AFTER JACKSON'S ARTILLERY BOMBARDED THEM FROM THE SURROUNDING HILLS, THE U.S. FORCE AT HARPERS FERRY SURRENDERED.

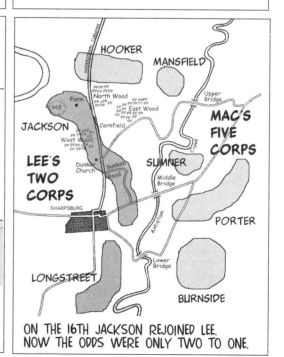

ON THE 16TH JACKSON REJOINED LEE. NOW THE ODDS WERE ONLY TWO TO ONE.

GEN. AMBROSE
POWELL HILL,
CSA

SEPTEMBER 17, 1862

POWELL HILL GOT ALL THE CAPTURED MEN AND SUPPLIES STARTED FOR RICHMOND AND BEGAN A FORCED MARCH TOWARD SHARPSBURG.

ON THE MARCH A.P. HILL RECEIVED A ONE-WORD MESSAGE FROM LEE.

THE BATTLE STARTED AT DAWN WHEN HOOKER'S CORPS CHARGED THROUGH THE CORNFIELD NORTH OF THE DUNKER CHURCH.

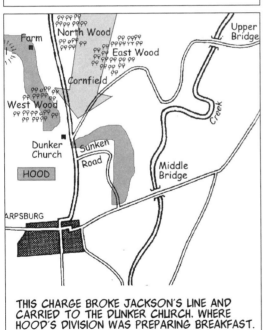

THIS CHARGE BROKE JACKSON'S LINE AND CARRIED TO THE DUNKER CHURCH. WHERE HOOD'S DIVISION WAS PREPARING BREAKFAST.

HOOD'S MEN HAD BEEN TAKEN OUT OF THE LINE TO GET THEIR FIRST MEAL IN DAYS. NOW THEY HAD TO STOP HOOKER.

THEY PUSHED THE YANKEES BACK THROUGH THE CORN FIELD TO THEIR ORIGINAL POSITION.

THE BREACH WAS CLOSED. BUT THE PRICE HAD BEEN HIGH.

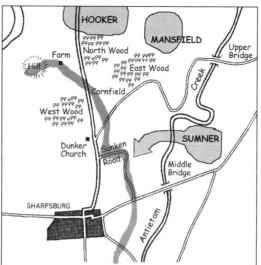

MANSFIELD HAD SUPPORTED HOOKER IN HIS FAILED ATTEMPT TO BREAK THROUGH THE REBEL LINE. NOW IT WAS SUMNER'S TURN. HE STORMED THE CONFEDERATE CENTER.

THE YANKEES WERE STOPPED BY HARVEY HILL'S DIVISION. SHELTERED BY THE SUNKEN ROAD, THE REBELS REPULSED REPEATED CHARGES.

FINALLY THE YANKEES REACHED A POSITION WHERE THEY COULD SHOOT DOWN INTO THE SUNKEN ROAD, FORCING THE REBELS TO PULL BACK.

SO MANY CONFEDERATE DEAD WERE LEFT IN THE SUNKEN ROAD THAT IT IS CALLED "BLOODY LANE" TO THIS DAY.

GENERAL LONGSTREET NOTICED A CANNON WHOSE CREW HAD ALL BEEN KILLED OR WOUNDED.

DISMOUNT, GENTLEMEN! WE'VE ALL HAD ARTILLERY TRAINING.

LONGSTREET CALLED ON HIS PERSONAL STAFF.

AND SO A CANNON MANNED BY ONE CAPTAIN, TWO MAJORS, AND ONE GENERAL HELPED STOP THE YANKEE ADVANCE.

OH, NO!

VOLUNTEER NURSE CLARA BARTON WAS TENDING TO A WOUNDED U.S. SOLDIER WHEN A BULLET WENT THROUGH HER SLEEVE AND KILLED HIM. AFTER THE WAR SHE FOUNDED THE AMERICAN RED CROSS.

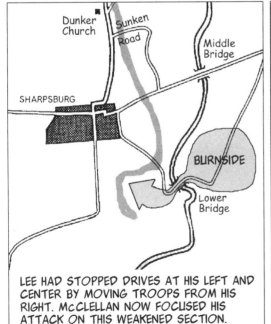

LEE HAD STOPPED DRIVES AT HIS LEFT AND CENTER BY MOVING TROOPS FROM HIS RIGHT. McCLELLAN NOW FOCUSED HIS ATTACK ON THIS WEAKENED SECTION.

UH-OH! THIS TIME THEY MEAN BUSINESS!

AFTER HOURS OF TRYING, GEN. BURNSIDE FINALLY SEIZED THE LOWER BRIDGE, NOW KNOWN AS BURNSIDE'S BRIDGE.

THE CONFEDERATE RIGHT FLANK WAS FORCED INTO THE TOWN OF SHARPSBURG.

JUST AS THE YANKEES THOUGHT THEY HAD WON, THEY WERE ATTACKED FROM THE SIDE BY A STRONG FORCE OF CONFEDERATES.

IT WAS POWELL HILL'S DIVISION, WHICH HAD BEEN MARCHING ALL DAY FROM HARPERS FERRY. THE C.S. MEN HAD EXCHANGED THEIR RAGS FOR CAPTURED NEW U.S. UNIFORMS. BUT THEIR FLAGS AND THE FAMOUS REBEL YELL TOLD WHICH SIDE THEY WERE ON.

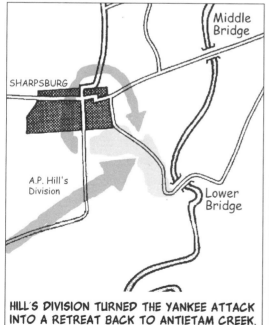

HILL'S DIVISION TURNED THE YANKEE ATTACK INTO A RETREAT BACK TO ANTIETAM CREEK.

LEE KEPT HIS FORCES IN PLACE ALL THE NEXT DAY. BUT EVEN THOUGH McCLELLAN RECEIVED THOUSANDS OF REINFORCEMENTS HE DID NOT RENEW THE BATTLE.

THE DAY OF THE BATTLE, SEPTEMBER 17, 1862, WAS THE DEADLIEST SINGLE DAY OF THE WAR. KILLED, WOUNDED, AND CAPTURED, THE U.S.A. CASUALTIES WERE 12,400; THOSE OF THE C.S.A. WERE 10,315; A TOTAL OF 22,715 AMERICANS.

ALTHOUGH THE BATTLE HAD BEEN A DRAW, LEE'S CASUALTIES HAD BEEN TOO HIGH TO PERMIT HIM TO CONTINUE HIS INVASION. HE WITH-DREW HIS MEN TO VIRGINIA WITH-OUT U.S. OPPOSITION.

DANIEL HARVEY HILL

AMBROSE POWELL HILL

LEE'S TWO HILLS AT SHARPSBURG

HARVEY HILL SAVED LEE'S ARMY AT THE BEGINNING BY HOLDING THE MOUNTAIN PASSES. AND POWELL HILL SAVED IT AT THE END BY HIS FORCED MARCH FROM HARPERS FERRY.

CHAPTER 11

THE EMANCIPATION PROCLAMATION

Free at Last?

MY PARAMOUNT OBJECT IN THIS STRUGGLE IS TO SAVE THE UNION, AND IS NOT EITHER TO SAVE OR DESTROY SLAVERY. IF I COULD SAVE THE UNION WITHOUT FREEING ANY SLAVE, I WOULD DO IT; AND IF I COULD SAVE IT BY FREEING ALL THE SLAVES, I WOULD DO IT; AND IF I COULD SAVE IT BY FREEING SOME AND LEAVING OTHERS ALONE, I WOULD ALSO DO THAT.

Abraham Lincoln

AUGUST 22, 1862 — LINCOLN WROTE AN OPEN LETTER TO NEWSPAPER PUBLISHER HORACE GREELEY.

LINCOLN DECIDED THAT HE COULD BEST ACHIEVE HIS GOAL OF PRESERVING THE UNION BY DOING THE LAST: HE WOULD FREE SOME SLAVES AND LEAVE OTHERS ALONE

I WANTED A BIG VICTORY TO RELEASE THIS, BUT ANTIETAM WILL HAVE TO DO.

ALTHOUGH THE BATTLE OF SHARPSBURG (ANTIETAM) HAD BEEN A DRAW, IT HAD FORCED LEE TO LEAVE UNION SOIL.

WELL, WHAT DO YOU THINK?

SEPTEMBER 22, 1862 — LINCOLN READS HIS PRELIMINARY EMANCIPATION PROCLAMATION TO HIS CABINET.

CALEB B. SMITH, SEC. OF THE INTERIOR

ONLY DICTATORSHIPS ARE GOVERNED BY EXECUTIVE PROCLAMATIONS.

WILLIAM H. SEWARD, SEC. OF STATE

LINCOLN KNEW NO FOREIGN NATION WANTED TO BE SEEN AS FAVORING SLAVERY.

SALMON P. CHASE, SEC. OF THE TREASURY

"HEREAFTER, AS BEFORE, THE WAR WILL BE FOUGHT FOR THE OBJECT OF RESTORING THE RELATION BETWEEN THE UNITED STATES AND EACH OF THE STATES."

MONTGOMERY BLAIR, POSTMASTER GENERAL

EDWIN M. STANTON, SECRETARY OF WAR

GIDEON WELLES, SEC. OF THE NAVY

AFTER THE WAR, WHAT WILL WE DO WITH ALL THE FREED NEGROES?

WE MUST PERSUADE THEM TO LEAVE THE COUNTRY.

EDWARD BATES, ATTORNEY GENERAL

LINCOLN WANTED TO EXPORT THE FREED SLAVES TO COLONIES IN AFRICA OR CENTRAL AMERICA.

ALTHOUGH THE PROCLAMATION DID NOT FREE A SINGLE SLAVE, LINCOLN KNEW THAT IT WOULD SEEM TO AND THAT, IN SEEMING TO, IT WOULD GIVE A NEW AND NOBLER PURPOSE TO THE WAR.

THOSE WEARY OF SACRIFICING SO MUCH JUST TO PREVENT THE SOUTH FROM BECOMING INDEPENDENT COULD NOW FEEL THAT THEY WERE FIGHTING TO EXPUNGE THE EVIL OF SLAVERY FROM AMERICAN SOIL. THIS GAVE NEW ENERGY AND PURPOSE TO THE NORTHERN EFFORT.

AFTER THE FIRST OF JANUARY, ONLY LOYAL AMERICANS CAN OWN SLAVES!

CHAPTER 12

FREDERICKSBURG
Lee vs. Burnside

I'M TIRED OF **STRUTTING PEACOCKS.** THIS TIME I WANT A **MODEST** MAN.

FOR TWO MONTHS AFTER THE BATTLE OF SHARPSBURG McCLELLAN FAILED TO MAKE AN AGGRESSIVE MOVE. SO LINCOLN DECIDED TO REPLACE HIM.

GEN. AMBROSE EVERETT BURNSIDE. USA

LINCOLN CHOSE GENERAL AMBROSE BURNSIDE. ALTHOUGH BURNSIDE WAS NOT SURE OF HIS OWN ABILITY TO COMMAND A LARGE ARMY, HE RELUCTANTLY ACCEPTED THE PROMOTION.

BURNSIDE DECIDED TO CROSS THE RAPPA-HANNOCK RIVER AT THE PICTURESQUE LITTLE TOWN OF FREDERICKSBURG. HALF WAY BETWEEN WASHINGTON AND RICHMOND.

THE CONFEDERATES HAD ALREADY DESTROYED THE FREDERICKSBURG BRIDGES.

WE'LL CROSS AS SOON AS THE PONTOONS GET HERE.

BUT THAT MAY GIVE THE REBS TIME TO OCCUPY THE TOWN!

ON NOVERMBER 17, 1862, BURNSIDE REACHED THE HEIGHTS ACROSS FROM FREDERICKSBURG. HE HAD ALREADY ORDERED PONTOON BRIDGES TO BE BROUGHT UP TO ALLOW HIS ARMY TO CROSS.

MY SCOUTS HAVE FOUND A FORD UPSTREAM WHERE WE CAN CROSS.

NO! THE RIVER COULD RISE AND TRAP PART OF THE ARMY ON THE OTHER BANK!

GEN. W.S. HANCOCK REPORTED TO BURNSIDE THAT THERE WAS A WAY TO GET THE ARMY ACROSS THE RAPPAHANNOCK RIVER BEFORE THE CONFEDERATES ARRIVED.

AT LEAST LET ME PUT MY DIVISION ACROSS AND SECURE THE TOWN.

NO! THE PONTOONS WILL ARRIVE AT ANY TIME AND WE CAN CROSS THE WAGONS AND CANNON AS WELL AS THE MEN.

BURNSIDE WOULD NOT DEVIATE FROM THE PLAN THAT HAD BEEN APPROVED BY WASHINGTON.

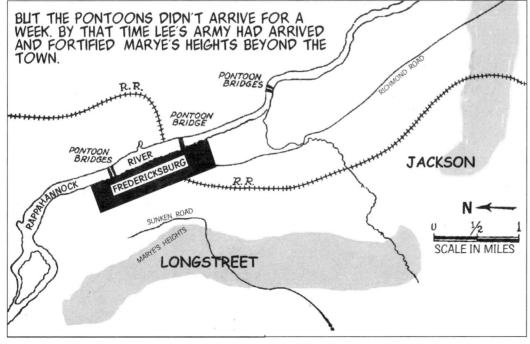

BUT THE PONTOONS DIDN'T ARRIVE FOR A WEEK. BY THAT TIME LEE'S ARMY HAD ARRIVED AND FORTIFIED MARYE'S HEIGHTS BEYOND THE TOWN.

R.R.

PONTOON BRIDGES

RICHMOND ROAD

PONTOON BRIDGE

PONTOON BRIDGES

RIVER

FREDERICKSBURG

RAPPAHANNOCK

R.R.

JACKSON

SUNKEN ROAD

MARYE'S HEIGHTS

LONGSTREET

N

0   ½   1

SCALE IN MILES

AS THE BATTLE APPROACHED THE TOWNSPEOPLE EVACUATED FREDERICKSBURG.

ON MARYE'S HEIGHTS GENERAL LEE GOT A REPORT FROM COLONEL ALEXANDER, HEAD OF ARTILLERY.

IN THE DARK OF NIGHT THE YANKEES MOVE THE PONTOON BOATS DOWN TO THE RIVER AND BEGIN TO ASSEMBLE THE BRIDGES.

A SMALL C.S. FORCE WAS STATIONED IN TOWN. BRIGADIER GENERAL WILLIAM BARKSDALE'S MISSISSIPPI BRIGADE.

BECAUSE OF BARKSDALE'S MEN THE U.S. ENGINEERS CONTINUALLY HAD TO RETREAT AND THEN SNEAK BACK TO WORK ON THE BRIDGE.

THURSDAY, DECEMBER 11, 1862

FOG CONCEALED THE BRIDGE BUILDERS UNTIL LATE THE FOLLOWING MORNING.

THE FOG LIFTED AND A HAIL OF BULLETS CUT DOWN THE ENGINEERS.

IN RESPONSE TO THE MISSISSIPPI SHARPSHOOTERS, THE BIG U.S. GUNS OPENED ON THE WATERFRONT AND TOWN.

GENERAL LEE SENT ME TO ASK IF YOU NEED ANYTHING.

NO. BUT TELL HIM I CAN BUILD HIM A BRIDGE OF DEAD YANKEES!

AN HOUR OF BOMBARDMENT HAD LITTLE EFFECT ON THE C.S. SOLDIERS, BUT IT BADLY DAMAGED THE TOWN.

USING PONTOON BOATS, A FORCE OF YANKEES CROSSED THE RIVER TO DRIVE THE SHARP-SHOOTERS AWAY FROM THE BANK.

GEN. LEE SAYS ABANDON THE TOWN!

JUST ONE MORE YANKEE AND I'LL CALL IT A DAY!

THE MISSISSIPPIANS RESISTED THE YANKEES BLOCK BY BLOCK. MEANWHILE THE BRIDGES WERE COMPLETED.

THE UNION OFFICERS PERMITTED THE SOLDIERS TO LOOT AND VANDALIZE THE ABANDONED HOMES.

SATURDAY, DECEMBER 13
THE U.S. TROOPS CROSS THE RAPPAHANNOCK INTO FREDERICKSBURG AND PREPARE FOR BATTLE.

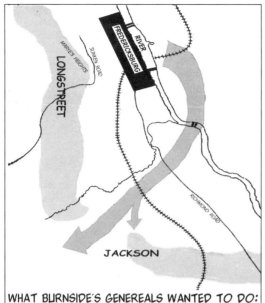

WHAT BURNSIDE'S GENEREALS WANTED TO DO: USE THE LOWER PONTOON BRIDGES TO HOLD OFF JACKSON WHILE FLANKING LONGSTREET.

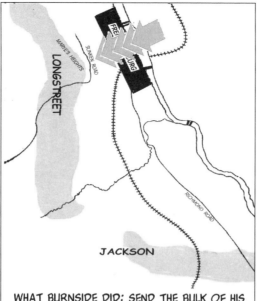

WHAT BURNSIDE DID: SEND THE BULK OF HIS ARMY PIECEMEAL AGAINST LONGSTREET'S IMPREGNABLE DEFENSES.

GEN. LONGSTREET, THE GREAT NUMBERS OF THOSE PEOPLE MAY OVERWHELM YOUR LINE!

GEN. LEE, LET EVERY YANKEE SOLDIER BETWEEN HERE AND WASHINGTON COME AT ME ACROSS THAT FIELD, AND I WILL KILL THEM ALL!

LONGSTREET WAS SURE HIS LINE WOULD HOLD.

HIS INFANTRY WAS FOUR DEEP BEHIND A STONE FENCE AT THE BOTTOM OF MARYE'S HEIGHTS, AND HIS ARTILLERY WAS ON TOP.

WAVE AFTER WAVE OF U.S. SOLDIERS BRAVELY CHARGED THE STONE WALL ONLY TO BE DECIMATED AND TURNED BACK.

WHAT? IRISHMEN FIGHTING AGAINST INDEPENDENCE?!

CHANCE HAD IT THAT THE U.S. IRISH BRIGADE WAS CUT TO PIECES BY A GEORGIA IRISH REGIMENT.

96

AS THE REMNANTS OF THE U.S. IRISH BRIGADE WITHDREW, THE C.S. IRISH CHEERED THEIR HEROISM.

THE FUTILE ASSAULTS CONTINUED ALL DAY. THE NEXT MORNING BURNSIDE WANTED TO RENEW THE ATTACK BUT HIS GENERALS REFUSED.

AS THEY RETREATED FROM FREDERICKSBURG, THE UNION TROOPS REFUSED TO CHEER GENERAL BURNSIDE.

LINCOLN REMOVED BURNSIDE FROM COMMAND OF THE ARMY OF THE POTOMAC BUT ALLOWED HIM TO REMAIN AS A DIVISION COMMANDER.

CHAPTER 13

STREIGHT ACROSS ALABAMA
How a Teen-Aged Girl Helped Her Country

THE REBEL CAVALRY RAIDS BEHIND OUR LINES ARE DISRUPTING OUR OFFENSIVE.

DON'T I KNOW IT!

MARCH, 1863
COL. ABEL STREIGHT MEETS WITH GEN. ROSECRANS, WHO COMMANDS THE UNITED STATES FORCES IN CENTRAL TENNESSEE.

I WANT TO DO TO THEM WHAT THEY'VE BEEN DOING TO US!

STREIGHT ASKED TO LEAD A RAID DEEP INTO CONFEDERATE TERRITORY.

"I'LL LEAD A BRIGADE OF MOUNTED INFANTRY FROM NASHVILLE DOWN THE CUMBERLAND AND THEN UP THE TENNESSEE TO JOIN GEN. DODGE AT EAST PORT, ALABAMA."

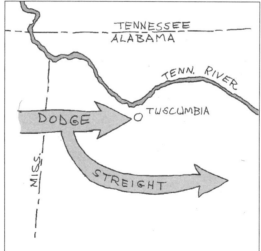

"HAVE GEN. DODGE MOVE ON TUSCUMBIA TO TIE DOWN THE REBEL CAVALRY WHILE MY BRIGADE SLIPS AWAY"

WE'LL MOVE SWIFTLY ACROSS ALABAMA AND DESTROY THE ARMAMENT FACTORIES AND RAILROADS IN NORTHWEST GEORGIA.

COL. STREIGHT HAD THOUGHT OF EVERYTHING. THE MOUNTAIN AREAS OF NORTHERN ALABAMA CONTAINED MANY WITH UNION SYMPATHIES.

STREIGHT ASSEMBLED HIS BRIDGADE. MULES WOULD BE USED BECAUSE THEY WERE MORE SURE-FOOTED AND REQUIRED LESS FOOD THAN HORSES.

WHEN THE MULES WERE UNLOADED AT EAST PORT THEY BEGAN TO MAKE A TREMENDOUS NOISE.

MILES AWAY CONFEDERATE SCOUTS HEARD THE HONKING OF THE MULES AND SET OUT TOWARD THE SOURCE OF THE NOISE.

THE SCOUTS SLIPPED AMONG THE MULES AND STARTED A STAMPEDE.

IT TOOK TWO DAYS FOR THE YANKEES TO ROUND THEM UP. AND ABOUT 200 WERE NOT RECOVERED.

WELL, WE'VE TAKEN TUSCUMBIA.

LET'S SEE HOW THE REBS REACT.

AS PLANNED, STREIGHT JOINED GEN. DODGE TO CAPTURE TUSCUMBIA.

MOVE UP, MEN, MOVE UP!

AS TUSCUMBIA FALLS TO THE U.S., BRIG. GEN. NATHAN BEDFORD FORREST IS SENT FROM TENNESSEE TO STRENGTHEN C.S. FORCES IN ALABAMA.

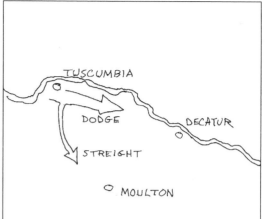

TUSCUMBIA

DODGE

DECATUR

STREIGHT

MOULTON

APRIL 19, 1863

WHEN STREIGHT HEARD THAT FORREST HAD CROSSED THE TENNESSEE RIVER HE SLIPPED AWAY FROM THE MAIN U.S. FORCE TO BEGIN HIS RAID.

THE YANKEES PULLED OUT AT DAWN!

WELL, THEY'RE TRYING TO FLANK DECATUR OR THEY'RE HEADED FOR GEORGIA.

WHEN FORREST LEARNED OF STREIGHT'S MOVEMENT HE LED HIS OWN BRIGADE TO MOULTON.

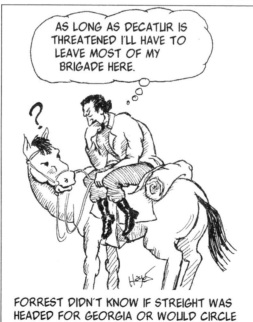

AS LONG AS DECATUR IS THREATENED I'LL HAVE TO LEAVE MOST OF MY BRIGADE HERE.

FORREST DIDN'T KNOW IF STREIGHT WAS HEADED FOR GEORGIA OR WOULD CIRCLE BACK ON DECATUR.

WE'VE DOUBLE-TEAMED THE GUNS AND CHECKED ALL THE HORSESHOES.

I'LL CHECK ALL THE HARNESSES MYSELF. ISSUE THREE DAYS RATIONS FOR HORSE AND MAN.

HE SELECTED THE FASTEST HORSES FOR THE PURSUIT OF STREIGHT AND LEFT THE REST OF HIS BRIGADE TO PROTECT DECATUR.

SOUTH OF MOULTON, STREIGHT FOUND HUNDREDS OF REFUGEES WITH THEIR LIVESTOCK AND BELONGINGS. HE SEIZED EVERYTHIG HE NEEDED.

FORREST CAUGHT UP WITH STREIGHT AT SAND MOUNTAIN, BUT HIS MEN STOPPED THEIR ADVANCE TO EAT THE BREAKFAST LEFT BY THE FLEEING YANKEES.

AS STREIGHT FLED, FORREST ORDERED COL. ANDERSON TO TAKE HIS REGIMENT NORTH TO KEEP THE ENEMY FROM ESCAPING THROUGH GUNTERSVILLE.

EVERY TIME FORREST CAUGHT UP WITH HIM, STREIGHT SACRIFICED A REAR GUARD TO ALLOW THE REST OF HIS COMMAND TO ESCAPE.

STREIGHT WAS GOOD AT LAYING AMBUSHES.

FORREST WAS GOOD AT DISCOVERING AMBUSHES.

FORREST HAD TO KEEP THE PRESSURE UP WITHOUT WEARING OUT HIS MEN.

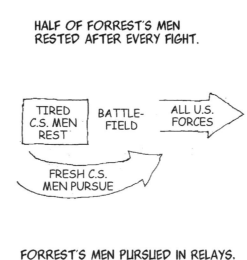

FORREST'S MEN PURSUED IN RELAYS. THE FRESHER MEN CATCHING UP WHEN THE YANKS TURNED TO FIGHT.

AT BLOUNTSVILLE, STREIGHT HAD THE BAGGAGE TRANSFERRED TO PACK MULES AND THE WAGONS BURNED.

FORREST ARRIVED IN TIME TO SALVAGE NEEDED SUPPLIES.

ALL ACROSS ALABAMA, FORREST PURSUED STREIGHT IN A SERIES OF FORCED FIGHTS.

FORREST TRIMMED HIS FORCES TO THE FITTEST SIX HUNDRED MEN AND HORSES.

HE CAUGHT UP AGAIN AT BLACK CREEK BUT THE YANKEES HAD BURNED THE BRIDGE BEHIND THEM.

FORREST SOUGHT INFORMATION AT A NEARBY FARMHOUSE.

SIXTEEN YEAR OLD EMMA SANSOM HAD A BETTER IDEA.

EMMA SCRAMBLED UP BEHIND THE GENERAL TO GUIDE HIM.

EMMA SHOWED THE GENERAL WHERE THE COWS WADED THE CREEK.

DISMOUNTING FOR A CLOSER LOOK. THEY CAME UNDER FIRE FROM THE U.S. REAR GUARD.

SOON FORREST'S MEN WERE CHARGING ACROSS EMMA'S FORD.

FORREST LEFT EMMA A HASTILY WRITTEN LETTER OF APPRECIATION.

THE GENERAL WAS SENSITIVE ABOUT HIS MEAGER EDUCATION. SO EMMA RECEIVED ONE OF THE FEW SURVIVING LETTERS IN FORREST'S OWN HAND.

Hed Quaters In Sadle
May 2, 1863

My highest Regardes to Miss Ema Sanson for hir gallant conduct while my forse was skirmishing with the Federals a cross Black Creek near Gadesden Allabama

N.B. Forrest
Brig Genl
Comding N. Ala--12

THE U.S. MEN BARELY HAD TIME TO BURN CONFEDERATE STORES IN GADSDEN BEFORE FORREST'S ADVANCE CAUGHT UP.

STREIGHT'S STAFF WAS GLOOMY BUT HE WASN'T.

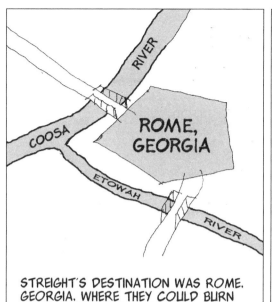

STREIGHT'S DESTINATION WAS ROME, GEORGIA, WHERE THEY COULD BURN THE BRIDGES BEHIND THEM.

ROME WAS AN IMPORTANT RAILROAD AND INDUSTRIAL CENTER.

STREIGHT SENT 200 MEN AHEAD TO SEIZE AND HOLD THE BRIDGE AT ROME.

ONE OF FORREST'S MEN WAS CAPTURED. HE TOLD A CONVINCING LIE.

STREIGHT ORDERED A FORCED NIGHT MARCH TOWARD ROME.

WHILE THE U.S. TROOPERS STAGGERED ON, FORREST'S MEN GOT A GOOD NIGHTS REST.

THE REFRESHED SOUTHERNERS TOOK ONLY FOUR HOURS TO CATCH UP WITH STREIGHT.

STREIGHT GOT BAD NEWS. SOME OF FORREST'S MEN HAD BEATEN HIS DETACHMENT TO ROME.

FORREST SENT A MESSAGE UNDER A FLAG OF TRUCE.

WHILE THE COMMANDERS TALKED STREIGHT SAW TWELVE CANNONS ROLL BY.

HE WAS COUNTING THE SAME TWO GUNS OVER AND OVER.

STREIGHT WAS SUSPICIOUS.

106

FORREST WAS FIRM.

STREIGHT'S OFFICERS CONVINCED HIM.

MAY 3, 1863

SO STREIGHT'S RAID ENDED WITH 1600 U.S. SOLDIERS SURRENDERING TO 500 CONFEDERATES.

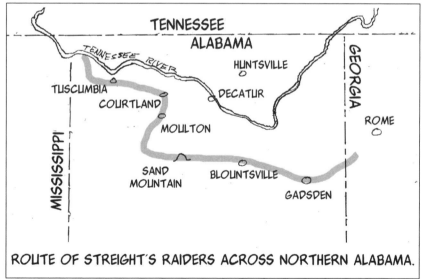

ROUTE OF STREIGHT'S RAIDERS ACROSS NORTHERN ALABAMA.

CHAPTER 14

CHANCELLORSVILLE
Lee vs. Hooker

WINTER OF 1862-63

BOTH THE U.S. ARMY OF THE POTOMAC AND THE C.S. ARMY OF NORTHERN VIRGINIA WINTERED NEAR FREDERICKSBURG. BUT LEE HAD TO SEND PART OF HIS ARMY SOUTH FOR PROVISIONS.

GEN. JOSEPH HOOKER, USA

LINCOLN REPLACED BURNSIDE WITH "FIGHTING" JOE HOOKER AS HEAD OF THE ARMY OF THE POTOMAC.

WILL THAT BE ALL, SIR?

DON'T BE STUFFY! SUGAR, POUR THE MAJOR A DRINK.

HOOKER'S FONDNESS FOR GAMBLING, DRINKING, AND WOMANIZING EMBARRASSED SOME OF HIS OFFICERS.

GENERAL HOOKER! HURRAH... HURRAH...**HURRAH!**

DESPITE HIS WANTON HABITS HE WAS A CAPABLE OFFICER AND SOON RESTORED THE SPIRIT OF HIS TROOPS.

WELL, I SAW ABOUT A THOUSAND REBS GO UP THE HILL AND LATER I SAW ABOUT THE SAME NUMBER COME DOWN.

THAT MAKES TWO THOUSAND.

MCCLELLAN HAD ALWAYS OVERESTIMATED THE NUMBER OF THE ENEMY BECAUSE HE HAD RELIED ON THE PINKERTON DETECTIVE AGENCY FOR HIS INFORMATION.

I CALCULATE THAT LEE NOW HAS 60,327 MEN, NOT COUNTING COOKS AND DRUMMER BOYS.

HOOKER FIRED PINKERTON AND CULTIVATED A NUMBER OF SPIES IN THE AREA. AS A RESULT HE KNEW LEE'S STRENGTH ALMOST EXACTLY.

GEN. GEORGE STONEMAN, USA

FOLLOWING LEE'S EXAMPLE, HOOKER POOLED MOST OF THE SMALL CAVALRY UNITS INTO A SINGLE COMMAND. HE PLACED JACKSON'S OLD WEST POINT ROOMMATE IN CHARGE OF THE NEW CORPS OF 10,000 TROOPERS.

WE'LL USE LEE'S OWN TACTICS AGAINST HIM — DIVIDE OUR FORCES AND OUTFLANK HIM!

APRIL 25, 1863
HOOKER EXPLAINS HIS PLAN TO HIS CORPS COMMANDERS.

YOU, GEN. STONEMAN, WILL TAKE YOUR CAVALRY SOUTH TO CUT OFF LEE'S SUPPLIES!

IT WOULD HAVE BEEN WISER TO KEEP THE CAVALRY NEAR THE SCENE OF THE APPROACHING BATTLE.

GEN. SEDGWICK, YOU WILL TAKE UP A POSITION FACING LEE AT FREDERICKSBURG.

SEDGWICK WAS TO KEEP LEE FROM SLIPPING AWAY TOWARD RICHMOND.

GEN. HOWARD, YOU WILL TAKE THE 11TH CORPS ON A WIDE SWEEP TO COME AT LEE FROM THE REAR!

GEN. OLIVER OTIS HOWARD HAD LOST HIS RIGHT ARM AT SEVEN PINES. HIS CORPS WAS MADE UP MOSTLY OF GERMAN IMMIGRANTS.

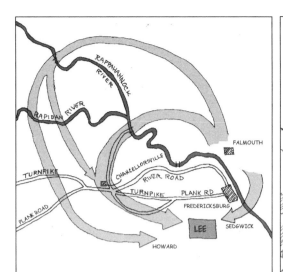

"WE'LL LEAVE A SMALL FORCE AT FALMOUTH TO FOOL LEE. AND THE REST OF THE ARMY WILL CONCENTRATE AT CHANCELLORSVILLE. REGROUP AND ATTACK FROM THREE DIRECTIONS."

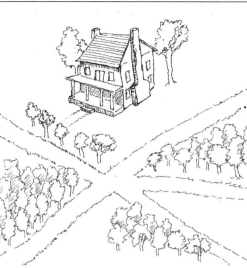

CHANCELLORSVILLE WAS NOT A TOWN. IT WAS A LARGE HOUSE AT A CROSSROADS IN AN AREA OF THICKETS CALLED "THE WILDERNESS."

MY PLANS ARE PERFECT. MAY GOD HAVE MERCY ON GEN. LEE. FOR I WILL HAVE NONE!

WHACK!

HOOKER WAS VERY CONFIDENT. HE HAD 130.000 MEN TO LEE'S 60.000 AND HE HAD WORKED OUT A PLAN TO TRAP AND DESTROY LEE'S ARMY.

GEN. JACKSON. I HAVE SENT FOR GEN. LONGSTREET. BUT YOU AND I MUST PROCEED ON THE ASSUMPTION THAT HE WILL NOT ARRIVE IN TIME.

MAY 1. 1863. LATE AT NIGHT

LEE WAS NOT DECEIVED. AT THE FIRST SIGN OF YANKEE MOVEMENT HE SHIFTED MOST OF HIS ARMY TOWARD CHANCELLORSVILLE.

GENERAL STUART INFORMS ME THAT THE YANKEE RIGHT FLANK IS 'IN THE AIR' – EXPOSED AND UNSUPPORTED.

THAT'S IT! YOU MUST TAKE YOUR CORPS AND OUTFLANK THE FLANKERS!

SITTING ON EMPTY CRACKER CRATES. LEE AND JACKSON WORKED OUT THEIR PLAN

IF I TAKE MY WHOLE CORPS YOU WON'T HAVE ENOUGH MEN TO RESIST HOOKER.

BUT HE WON'T KNOW THAT IF YOU CAN MOVE UNSEEN. **SECRECY IS CRUCIAL**!

IT WAS A BOLD PLAN.

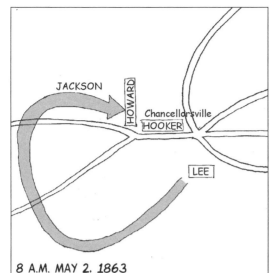

8 A.M. MAY 2, 1863

LED BY A LOCAL GUIDE. JACKSON'S COLUMN STARTS OUT ON A CIRCUITOUS ROUTE TO OUTFLANK THE ENEMY.

ON HIS WAY JACKSON FOUND LEE WAITING TO WISH HIM GODSPEED. IT WAS TO BE THE LAST TIME THESE GREAT WARRIORS MET.

SECRECY AND SILENCE WERE THE WATCH-WORDS FOR THE MARCH.

5 P.M., MAY 2, 1863

THE MEN OF GEN. HOWARD'S CORPS WERE PREPARING THEIR EVENING MEAL. THEIR RIFLES STACKED. THEIR CANNONS UNMANNED AND FACING THE WRONG DIRECTION.

OUT OF THE WOODS SURGED AN IRRESISTIBLE TIDE OF REBELS, OVERRUNNING HOWARD'S CORPS ONE DIVISION AFTER ANOTHER.

AS NIGHT FELL JACKSON URGED HIS MEN FORWARD TO CUT THE ENEMY OFF FROM THE RIVER FORDS.

BUT THE DIFFERENT UNITS HAD BECOME SO CONFUSED IN THE TANGLE OF WOODS THAT A NIGHT ATTACK WAS IMPOSSIBLE.

RETURNING TOWARD THE CONFEDERATE LINES, JACKSON'S PARTY WAS MISTAKEN FOR THE ENEMY BY THEIR OWN SOLDIERS.

HIS STAFF TRIED TO KEEP THE ARMY FROM LEARNING THAT JACKSON WAS SERIOUSLY WOUNDED.

FROM THE MEDICAL STATION JACKSON WAS TAKEN BY AMBULANCE TO A FIELD HOSPITAL.

THE BATTLE RESUMED THE NEXT MORNING WITH JEB STUART TEMPORARILY IN COMMAND OF JACKSON'S CORPS.

ON THE PORCH OF THE CHANCELLOR HOUSE HOOKER WAS WATCHING HIS "PERFECT" PLAN UNRAVEL WHEN A CANNON BALL STRUCK THE PILLAR HE WAS LEANING AGAINST.

HE WAS TOO ADDLED TO CONTINUE TO COMMAND. HIS LAST ORDER WAS FOR A GENERAL RETREAT, GIVING LEE THE VICTORY.

AFTER THE AMPUTATION, JACKSON WAS MOVED TO A PRIVATE HOME, WHERE HE SEEMED TO BE RECOVERING.

HIS WIFE ANNA CAME AND BROUGHT THEIR INFANT DAUGHTER TO CHEER HIM UP.

ANNA WANTED THE TRUTH.

MAY 10, 1863

JACKSON LAY DYING. HE BECAME DELIRIOUS AND IMAGINED HE WAS COMMANDING A BATTLE. THEN HE GREW QUIET AND SMILED.

JACKSON'S LAST WORDS.

CHAPTER 15

VICKSBURG
Splitting the South

WITH NEW ORLEANS SECURED GRANT WAS ASSIGNED THE TASK OF FREEING THE REST OF THE MISSISSIPPI RIVER.

If I thought this war was to abolish slavery, I would resign my commsission and offer my sword to the other side.

Ulysses S. Grant

GRANT, LIKE MOST U.S. SOLDIERS, WAS FIGHTING TO PRESERVE THE UNION, NOT TO FREE THE SLAVES.

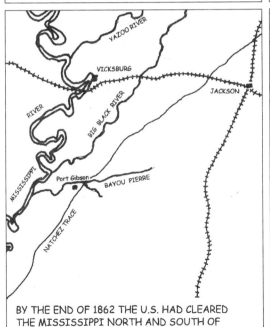

BY THE END OF 1862 THE U.S. HAD CLEARED THE MISSISSIPPI NORTH AND SOUTH OF VICKSBURG.

ANOTHER BLUE COAT BITES THE MUD!

HEAVILY FORTIFIED VICKSBURG WITH ITS HIGH BLUFFS REMAINED THE LAST OBSTACLE IN THE PLAN TO CLOSE THE MISSISSIPPI TO THE REBELS.

GENERAL JOHN C. PEMBERTON, CSA

AT VICKSBURG PEMBERTON COMMANDED 30,000 TROOPS. HIS BOSS WAS GEN. JOE JOHNSTON, RECOVERED FROM HIS PENINSULA WOUND AND NOW COMMANDING ALL WESTERN FORCES.

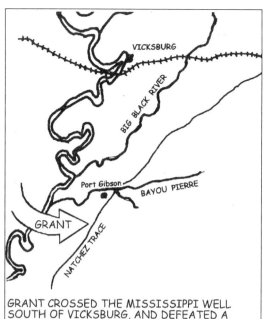

GRANT CROSSED THE MISSISSIPPI WELL SOUTH OF VICKSBURG, AND DEFEATED A SMALL CONFEDERATE FORCE AT PORT GIBSON

MAY 1, 1863 - PORT GIBSON, MISSISSIPPI, IS SAVED FROM DESTRUCTION BY GRANT'S WHIM.

JOHNSTON GATHERED A FORCE AT JACKSON AND ORDERED PEMBERTON TO MEET HIM THERE.

ONE OF GEN. JOHNSTON'S COURIERS WAS A SPY FOR GRANT. SO GRANT KNEW GENERAL PEMBERTON'S ORDERS BEFORE HE DID.

PEMBERTON WAS RELUCTANT TO LEAVE VICKSBURG UNDEFENDED, SO HE MOVED EASTWARD ONLY AS FAR AS CHAMPION'S HILL.

MOVING SWIFTLY, GRANT WAS ABLE TO DEFEAT JOHNSTON, DESTROY THE CITY OF JACKSON, AND THEN TURN AND DEFEAT PEMBERTON AT CHAMPION'S HILL.

DESPITE JOHNSTON'S ORDERS NOT TO LET HIS ARMY GET TRAPPED, PEMBERTON WITHDREW INTO VICKSBURG.

THE VICKSBURG DEFENDERS BEAT BACK REPEATED ASSAULTS BY THE FEDERALS.

AFTER REPEATED FAILED ASSAULTS, THE LAND BETWEEN THE LINES WAS STREWN WITH FEDERAL DEAD AND WOUNDED.

AFTER THREE DAYS THE REBELS ASK FOR A TRUCE SO THAT THE FEDERALS CAN TREAT THE FEW WOUNDED REMAINING ALIVE.

THE SIEGE OF VICKSBURG

GRANT WAS UNABLE TO CAPTURE VICKSBURG BY ASSAULT SO HE LAID SEIGE, CLOSING OFF ALL SUPPLIES, AND SUBJECTING BOTH MILITARY AND CIVILIAN TARGETS TO CONTINUAL ARTILLERY FIRE.

DAY AND NIGHT BOMBARDMENT OF THE CITY FORCED MANY FAMILIES TO DIG SHELTERS.

117

THE SOLDIERS WERE DOWN TO ONE BISCUIT AND ONE SMALL SLICE OF BACON PER DAY.

THE CIVILIAN POPULATION WAS ALSO SUFFERING GREAT HARDSHIP.

JULY 4, 1863 - PEMBERTON SURRENDERS VICKSBURG TO GRANT. THE VICTORIOUS YANKS SHARE THEIR RATIONS WITH THE HALF-STARVED DEFENDERS.

LINCOLN WAS GRATEFUL FOR THE VICTORY. THE SOUTH WAS NOW CUT IN TWO.

THE CITIZENS WERE SO EMBITTERED BY THEIR ORDEAL THAT THE FOURTH OF JULY WOULD NOT AGAIN BE CELEBRATED IN VICKSBURG FOR THREE GENERATIONS.

CHAPTER 16

GETTYSBURG
Lee vs. Meade

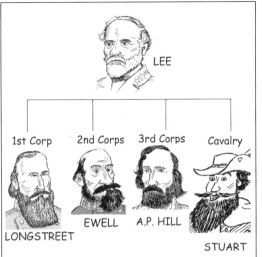

LEE REORGANIZED THE ARMY OF NORTHERN VIRGINIA INTO THREE CORPS, PROMOTING GEN. EWELL TO LEAD JACKSON'S OLD SECOND CORPS AND FORMING A NEW CORPS UNDER POWELL HILL.

MR. PRESIDENT, I FEAR THAT WE WILL LOSE UNLESS WE CAN BRING THIS WAR TO AN END SOON.

YOU MUST TAKE THE WAR TO THE ENEMY AGAIN!

FOLLOWING THE BATTLE OF CHANCELLORSVILLE, GENERAL LEE AND PRESIDENT DAVIS DECIDED ON A NEW INVASION OF THE UNITED STATES.

WHERE TO THIS TIME?

BOSTON, I HOPE!

JUST SO WE GET IT OVER WITH!

JUNE 3, 1863

THE ARMY OF NORTHERN VIRGINIA BEGINS TO MOVE NORTH. TO KEEP FROM BLOCKING THE ROADS, DIFFERENT DIVISIONS WOULD LEAVE AT DIFFERENT TIMES BY VARIOUS ROUTES.

JUNE 9, 1863: THE BATTLE OF BRANDY STATION STUART WAS SURPRISED BY THE U.S. CAVALRY, RESULTING IN THE LARGEST MOUNTED ENGAGEMENT OF THE WAR.

BAH! I'LL SHOW THEM!

ALTHOUGH HE WON THE BATTLE, STUART'S PRIDE WAS HURT BY WIDESPREAD CRITICISM. HE DECIDED TO RESTORE HIS TARNISHED FAME.

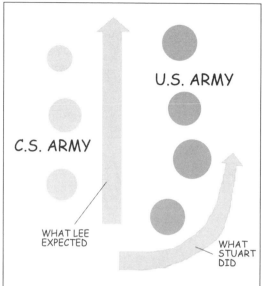

HE EMBARKED ON SOMETHING MORE DARING THAN THE JOB OF SCREENING THE ARMY AS IT MOVED. HE WOULD RIDE AROUND THE ENEMY, RAIDING AS HE WENT.

LEFT WITHOUT SUFFICIENT CAVALRY FOR EFFECTIVE SCREENING AND SCOUTING, LEE WAS "BLIND" TO THE POSITION AND STRENGTH OF THE ENEMY.

LINCOLN DECIDED TO REPLACE HOOKER. HE WAS STILL LOOKING FOR A GENERAL WHO COULD DEFEAT LEE.

GENERAL GEORGE GORDON MEADE

LINCOLN CHOSE MEADE, ONE OF HOOKER'S CORPS COMMANDERS, AS NEW HEAD OF THE ARMY OF THE POTOMAC.

JUNE 30, 1863

AFTER ENTERING PENNSYLVANIA, GEN. HETH OF HILL'S CORPS, HEARD THAT A SUPPLY OF SHOES WAS STORED AT GETTYSBURG AND SENT A BRIGADE TO SECURE THEM.

THE BRIGADE COMMANDER REPORTED BACK TO GENERAL HETH THAT A BRIGADE OF U.S. CAVALRY WAS OCCUPYING GETTYSBURG.

10 A.M., JULY 1, 1863 – THE FIRST DAY

HETH'S DIVISION ARRIVED AT GETTYSBURG AND FOUND THAT THE U.S. CAVALRY BRIGADE HAD BEEN JOINED BY AN INFANTRY DIVISION THAT INCLUDED THE FAMED IRON BRIGADE.

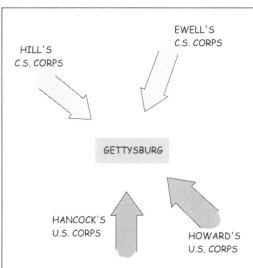

MORE REINFORCEMENTS FROM BOTH ARMIES NOW STREAMED TOWARD GETTYSBURG, AND THE GREATEST BATTLE OF THE WAR HAD BEGUN.

BY 5 P.M. THE CONFEDERATES HAD DRIVEN THE YANKEES OUT OF GETTYSBURG ONTO THE HEIGHTS SOUTH OF TOWN.

EWELL, COMMANDING JACKSON'S OLD SECOND CORPS, WAS STRUCK IN THE LEG BY A SHARP-SHOOTER'S BULLET.

EWELL HAD SO FAR BEEN A GOOD REPLACEMENT FOR JACKSON, BUT AT THIS CRITICAL MOMENT HE HESITATED.

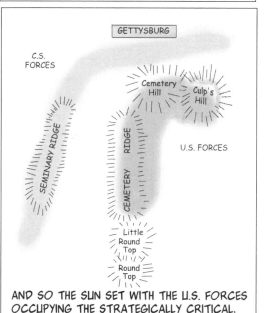

AND SO THE SUN SET WITH THE U.S. FORCES OCCUPYING THE STRATEGICALLY CRITICAL, HOOK-SHAPED HIGH GROUND.

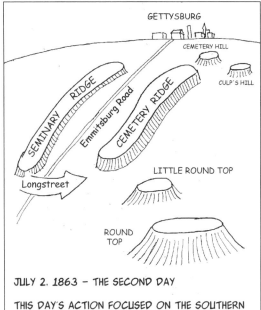

JULY 2, 1863 — THE SECOND DAY

THIS DAY'S ACTION FOCUSED ON THE SOUTHERN END OF MEADE'S DEPLOYMENT.

11:00 A.M. — IF LONGSTREET COULD HAVE STARTED SOONER HE WOULD HAVE FOUND BOTH ROUND TOPS UNOCCUPIED...

...BUT NOW COL. LAWRENCE CHAMBERLAIN AND HIS 20TH MAINE REGIMENT OCCUPIED THE CREST OF LITTLE ROUND TOP WITH ORDERS TO HOLD AT ALL COST.

THE MAINE MEN FOUGHT OFF REPEATED ATTACKS. FINALLY THEIR AMMUNITION WAS ALMOST USED UP.

THE SOUTHERNERS WERE SO STARTLED BY THE UNEXPECTED BAYONET CHARGE THAT THEY WERE ROUTED.

STUART FINALLY SHOWED UP. HIS TROOPERS TOO LATE AND TOO WORN OUT TO BE OF MUCH HELP.

JULY 3, 1863 — THE THIRD DAY

EWELL'S INDECISION ON THE FIRST DAY AND LONG-STREET'S SLOWNESS ON THE SECOND HAD LEFT MEADE'S ARMY IN A STRONG POSITION. NEVERTHELESS LEE DETERMINED ON A DESPERATE RISK.

LONGSTREET PROTESTED THE ATTACK BUT LEE INSISTED THAT HE COMMAND IT.

LONGSTREET WAS SO SURE THAT THE ATTACK WOULD FAIL THAT HE COULDN'T BRING HIMSELF TO GIVE THE ORDER. WHEN ASKED BY PICKETT HE COULD ONLY NOD.

IT IS CALLED PICKETT'S CHARGE AFTER THE COMMANDER OF THE LEAD DIVISION. BUT GENERAL LEWIS ARMISTEAD ACTUALLY LED. PINNING HIS HAT ON HIS SWORD AND HOLDING IT LIKE A FLAG.

IT WAS FREDERICKSBURG IN REVERSE. THIS TIME WITH THE YANKEES ON HIGH GROUND. FOUR DEEP BEHIND A STONE WALL.

GENERAL ARMISTEAD DID INDEED MAKE IT ALL THE WAY TO THE TOP. BUT IMMEDIATELY FELL, MORTALLY WOUNDED.

THE "HIGH TIDE OF THE CONFEDERACY" WAS PICKETT'S FAILED CHARGE.

LEE REPEATEDLY APOLOGIZED TO THE SURVIVORS AS THEY CAME BACK DOWN THE SLOPE.

THE CONFEDERATE CASUALTIES WERE SO GREAT THAT LEE WAS FORCED TO RETREAT.

MEADE FAILED TO FOLLOW UP HIS VICTORY, AND ALLOWED LEE'S ARMY TO ESCAPE BACK INTO VIRGINIA.

124

CHAPTER 17

TOTAL WAR
Grant Takes Command

THE FIRST CASUALTY OF THE WAR WAS THE UNITED STATES CONSTITUTION.

OVER 13,000 U.S. POLITICAL PRISONERS WERE HELD WITHOUT BENEFIT OF LAWYERS, TRIALS OR WRITS OF HABEUS CORPUS.

THE CONSTITUTION OF THE UNITED STATES OF AMERICA

Article IV
Section 3

...no new State shall be formed or erected within the Jurisdiction of any other State; nor any State be formed by the Junction of two or more States, or parts of States, without the the Consent of the Legislatures of the States concerned as well as of the Congress.

THE CONSTITUTION CLEARLY FORBIDS BREAKING AN EXISTING STATE INTO TWO STATES WITHOUT ITS CONSENT. AND YET...

JUNE 20, 1863

THE U.S. GOVERNMENT ADMITS WEST VIRGINIA INTO THE UNION AS A NEW STATE.

AT THE BEGINNING OF THE WAR U.S. GENERALS SUCH AS McCLELLAN AND BUELL RESTRAINED THEIR SOLDIERS FROM MISTREATING SOUTHERN CIVILIANS. BUT AS THE WAR CONTINUED AND SOUTHERNERS REMAINED LOYAL TO THE CONFEDERACY, THE LINCOLN ADMINISTRATION GREW CALLOUS TOWARD THEM.

THE NEW TONE WAS SET IN THE SPRING OF 1862 IN ATHENS, ALABAMA.

RUSSIAN COSSACK IVAN TURCHANINOV, A COLONEL IN THE CZAR'S ARMY, IMMIGRATED TO AMERICA IN 1856 AND AMERICANIZED HIS NAME TO JOHN TURCHIN.

NOW SERVING AS A U.S. COLONEL IN GENERAL DON CARLOS BUELL'S ARMY OF THE OHIO, TURCHIN COMMANDED A BRIGADE OCCUPYING NORTHERN ALABAMA.

ONE OF TURCHIN'S REGIMENTS WAS DRIVEN OUT OF ATHENS BY REBEL CAVALRY. THE TOWNSPEOPLE CHEERED THE CONFEDERATE SOLDIERS, AND SOME TOOK UP ARMS TO HELP THEM.

WHEN THE YANKEES MOVED BACK INTO ATHENS, TURCHIN DECIDED TO PUNISH THE TOWN BY GIVING HIS MEN PERMISSION TO PILLAGE.

THE YANKEE SOLDIERS LOOTED STORES AND HOMES AND TOOK WHATEVER THEY WANTED.

GEN. DON CARLOS BUELL HAD COL. TURCHIN COURTMARTIALED. HE WAS FOUND GUILTY AND HIS COMMISSION WAS REVOKED.

WE NEED MORE TURCHINS AND FEWER BUELLS.

LINCOLN INTERVENED FOR TURCHIN. OVERTURNING THE COURTMARTIAL AND PROMOTING HIM TO BRIGADIER GENERAL. IT WAS NOW CLEAR WHAT LINCOLN'S POLICY WOULD BE.

After Meade defeated Lee at Gettysburg, Lincoln thought he had at last found the right general. But Meade failed to follow up his win by destroying the Army of Northern Virginia.

WHY CAN'T I FIND A COMMANDER WHO WILL KEEP AFTER LEE UNTIL HIS ARMY IS DESTROYED?!

LINCOLN WAS DISGUSTED WITH MEADE.

WHAT WOULD YOU DO IF YOU WHIPPED LEE?

FIGHT HIM AGAIN IMMEDIATELY.

AND WHAT IF HE WHIPPED YOU?

FIGHT HIM AGAIN IMMEDIATELY.

LINCOLN INTERVIEWED GRANT AND AT LAST FOUND SOMEONE WHO AGREED WITH HIS HIS OWN VIEWPOINT.

WE HAVE SO MANY MORE MEN THAN THE REBELS THAT WE CAN LOSE ALL THE BATTLES AND STILL WIN THE WAR.

PROVIDED WE JUST KEEP FORCING BATTLES.

LINCOLN PUT GRANT IN CHARGE OF ALL UNION FORCES.

GEN. WILLIAM TECUMSEH SHERMAN

GRANT MADE SHERMAN COMMANDER IN THE WEST.

GEN. PHILIP SHERIDAN

GRANT GAVE SHERIDAN A JOB TO DO IN THE SHENANDOAH VALLEY.

BURN THE FARMERS OUT SO THE REBELS CAN'T GET SUPPLIES.

WHEN I GET DONE, A CROW WON'T BE ABLE TO CROSS THE VALLEY UNLESS HE CARRIES HIS OWN PROVISIONS!

SHERIDAN HAD THE RIGHT ATTITUDE.

I'LL LEAVE THEM NOTHING BUT THEIR EYES TO WEEP WITH.

LINCOLN, GRANT, SHERMAN, AND SHERIDAN ALL BELIEVED IN TOTAL WAR.

HE'S SOMEHOW ALWAYS BETWEEN ME AND ATLANTA.

IN THE WEST, SHERMAN'S ADVANCE WAS CONTINUALLY THWARTED BY GENERAL JOSEPH E. JOHNSTON'S SMALLER ARMY.

JOHNSTON WON'T FIGHT. I'M REPLACING HIM WITH HOOD.

PRESIDENT DAVIS COMMITTED A SERIOUS BLUNDER.

GENERAL JOHN BELL HOOD

HOOD WAS A VALIANT WARRIOR, BUT TOO RECKLESS TO COMMAND AN ARMY. MOREOVER, HE HAD LOST A LEG AND THE USE OF ONE ARM, AND WAS IN CONSTANT PAIN.

THROUGH COSTLY AND FRUITLESS BATTLES WITH SHERMAN, HOOD SOON LOST TOO MANY MEN TO CONTINUE TO DEFEND ATLANTA.

ABANDONING GEORGIA, HOOD MARCHED HIS WITHERED ARMY TOWARD NASHVILLE.

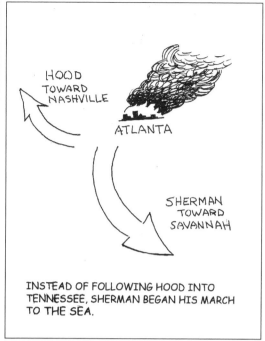

INSTEAD OF FOLLOWING HOOD INTO TENNESSEE, SHERMAN BEGAN HIS MARCH TO THE SEA.

SHERMAN'S ARMY LIVED BY PLUNDER, DESTROYING WHAT IT COULDN'T USE.

A LETTER FROM HOME.

LINCOLN'S POLICY AS PRACTICED BY SHERMAN LED TO MANY DESERTIONS FROM LEE'S ARMY.

129

CHAPTER 18

THE DAHLGREN RAID
Soldiers or Assassins?

DECEMBER 8, 1863 ANOTHER PROCLAMATION

LINCOLN OFFERED AMNESTY FOR MOST CONFEDERATES IF THEY WOULD TAKE AN OATH OF LOYALTY TO THE UNION. LACK OF RESPONSE MADE HIM WONDER IF WORD OF HIS PROCLAMATION WAS GETTING TO SOUTHERNERS.

THEY JUST HAVE TO SWEAR THAT THE UNION IS INDIVISIBLE.

SENATOR, WHILE THE REBS ARE IN WINTER CAMP I COULD EASILY SEIZE RICHMOND!

I'LL TALK TO THE PRESIDENT.

BRIG. GEN. JUDSON KILPATRICK WAS A FIERY CAVALRY OFFICER ALWAYS LOOKING FOR A CHANCE TO INCREASE HIS FAME. IN JANUARY, 1864, HE WAS IN WASHINGTON TALKING UP A PLAN FOR A CAVALRY RAID ON THE CONFEDERATE CAPITAL.

DO YOU THINK YOU COULD FREE THE THOUSANDS OF PRISONERS THERE?

SURE! AND I WILL SPREAD YOUR AMNESTY FLYERS EVERYWHERE!

FEB 12, 1864
WORD OF KILPATRICK'S PLAN REACHED LINCOLN, WHO SENT FOR HIM.

THE STATED OBJECTIVES OF THE RAID WILL BE: (1) FREE THE PRISONERS, (2) DESTROY COMMUN-ICATIONS, AND (3) DISTRIBUTE THE AMNESTY POSTERS.

WHAT ABOUT *UNSTATED* OBJECTIVES?

LINCOLN APPROVED KILPATRICK'S PLAN AND SENT HIM TO SECRETARY OF WAR STANTON TO WORK OUT THE DETAILS.

WELL, ONCE YOU TAKE RICHMOND YOU MIGHT AS WELL... (WHISPER, WHISPER)

YOU BET! AND WE COULD ALSO...(WHISPER, WHISPER)

THE OFFICIALLY STATED OBJECTIVES WERE NOT THE ONLY REASONS FOR THE RAID.

WHILE PREPARATIONS FOR THE RAID WERE UNDERWAY. A YOUNG COLONEL SHOWED UP AT KILPATRICK'S HEADQUARTERS.

KILPATRICK AND DAHLGREN SOON BECAME FRIENDS.

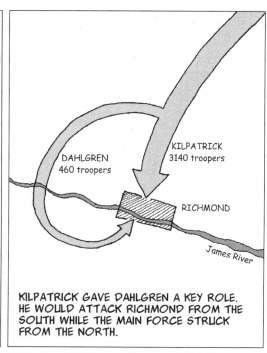

KILPATRICK GAVE DAHLGREN A KEY ROLE. HE WOULD ATTACK RICHMOND FROM THE SOUTH WHILE THE MAIN FORCE STRUCK FROM THE NORTH.

FEBRUARY 28. 1864

THE RAID BEGAN. KILPATRIC AND DAHLGREN LED 3600 CAVALRY TROOPERS TOWARD RICHMOND.

WHEN DAHLGREN SPLIT OFF FROM THE MAIN FORCE HE FOUND THE JAMES RIVER FLOODED AND COULD NOT CROSS. A FREE BLACK MAN OFFERED TO HELP.

WHEN THE GUIDE COULD NOT FIND A USABLE FORD. DAHLGREN SUSPECTED TREACHERY AND HAD HIM HANGED.

BUT KILPATRICK FOUND RICHMOND'S DEFENCES STRONGER THAN EXPECTED AND WITHDREW BEFORE DAHLGREN COULD JOIN HIM.

THE NIGHT OF MARCH 2, 1864

MOST OF DAHLGREN'S COMMAND MADE IT TO UNION LINES. BUT DAHLGREN AND ABOUT 100 OF HIS TROOPERS FELL INTO AN AMBUSH SET BY REBEL CAVALRY AND HOME GUARDS.

THE REBELS CALLED HIS BLUFF.

THE HOME GUARD COMPANY WAS COMMANDED BY A SCHOOL TEACHER, EDWARD HALBACH. ONE OF HIS "MEN" WAS A 13 YEAR-OLD STUDENT, WILLIAM LITTLEPAGE.

THE NEXT MORNING HALBACH READ THE CAPTURED DOCUMENTS. HE HURRIED THE PAPERS ON TO RICHMOND.

"...The city...must be destroyed & Jeff Davis and Cabinet killed."

"Jeff Davis and Cabinet must be killed on the spot."

EXCERPTS FROM THE DAHLGREN PAPERS.

IN RICHMOND COPIES OF THE DOCUMENTS WERE GIVEN TO THE NEWSPAPERS. SOON EVERYONE WAS READING ABOUT THE STORY.

IN THE CITY OF WASHINGTON. ONE YOUNG ACTOR TOOK THE MATTER VERY SERIOUSLY. HIS NAME WAS JOHN WILKES BOOTH.

CHAPTER 19

THE FINAL BATTLES
The Confederacy's Last Days

NEAR NASHVILLE AT FRANKLIN, HOOD LOST THE LAST HOPE FOR THE CONFEDERACY IN DOOMED ASSAULTS ON ENTRENCHED YANKS.

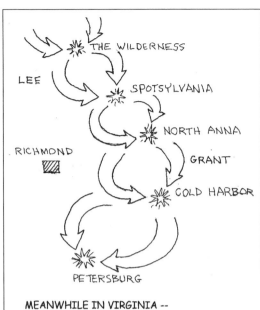

MEANWHILE IN VIRGINIA --
LEE SOMEHOW KEPT HIS DWINDLING ARMY BETWEEN GRANT AND RICHMOND.

MAY 9, 1864
SPOTSYLVANIA

AS THE ARMIES READY FOR BATTLE, CONFEDERATE SNIPERS GO TO WORK AT LONG RANGE.

DON'T WORRY BOYS, THEY COULDN'T HIT AN ELEPHANT AT THIS DISTANCE!

POPULAR UNION GENERAL "UNCLE" JOHN SEDGWICK JOKINGLY REASSURES HIS MEN.

THESE ARE HIS LAST WORDS. HE IS IMMEDIATELY STRUCK AND KILLED BY A SNIPER'S BULLET.

BOTH ARMIES WERE SUFFERING HEAVY CASUALTIES, BUT ONLY GRANT'S WAS RECEIVING REPLACEMENTS.

AT PETERSBURG, LEE DUG IN AND GRANT LAID SEIGE.

GENERAL BURNSIDE HAD A PLAN TO BREAK THROUGH.

AS PLANNED, THE EXPLOSION KILLED MANY REBELS AND MADE AN OPENING IN THEIR LINE.

BUT WHEN THE YANKEES CHARGED THEY FOUND THEMSELVES TRAPPED IN THE EXPLOSION CRATER.

BURNSIDE WAS DISGRACED, AND THE SIEGE RESUMED.

WHEN GRANT FINALLY SUCCEEDED IN CUTTING OFF ALL SUPPLIES INTO PETERSBURG, LEE HAD TO ABANDON THE CITY.

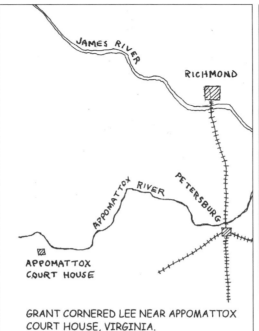

GRANT CORNERED LEE NEAR APPOMATTOX COURT HOUSE, VIRGINIA.

THERE WAS NOTHING LEFT BUT TO SURRENDER.

LEE BADE FAREWELL TO HIS GALLANT ARMY.

"YOU WILL TAKE WITH YOU THE SATISFACTION THAT PROCEEDS FROM THE CONSCIOUSNESS OF DUTY FAITHFULLY PERFORMED, AND I EARNESTLY PRAY THAT A MERCIFUL GOD WILL EXTEND TO YOU HIS BLESSING AND PROTECTION. WITH AN INCREASING ADMIRATION OF YOUR CONSTANCY AND DEVOTION TO YOUR COUNTRY ... I BID YOU ALL AN AFFECTIONATE FAREWELL."

Robert E. Lee
April 10, 1865

A FEW DAYS AFTER LEE'S SURRENDER, PRESIDENT AND MRS. LINCOLN ATTENDED A PLAY AT FORD'S THEATER IN WASHINGTON.

THE ACTOR, JOHN WILKES BOOTH, SLIPPED INTO THE PRESIDENTIAL BOX AND FIRED ONE PISTOL SHOT INTO THE BACK OF LINCOLN'S HEAD.

BOOTH LEAPED TO THE STAGE. HIS RIGHT SPUR CAUGHT IN BUNTING, CAUSING HIM TO BREAK HIS LEFT LEG.

*SIC SEMPER TYRANNIS!

*WHAT BRUTUS SAID WHEN HE SLEW CAESAR, "THUS ALWAYS TO TYRANTS!."

BOOTH STOOD UP AND DELIVERED HIS FINAL LINE FROM STAGE. THEN HE HOBBLED OFF TO BE CAUGHT AND KILLED TEN DAYS LATER.

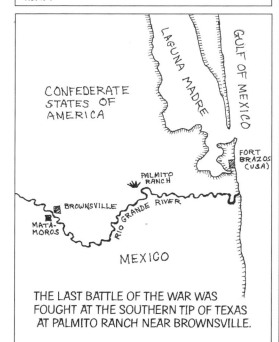

THE LAST BATTLE OF THE WAR WAS FOUGHT AT THE SOUTHERN TIP OF TEXAS AT PALMITO RANCH NEAR BROWNSVILLE.

ME AND GRANDPAW WANT TO ENLIST!

SO MANY TEXAS RANGERS HAD LEFT FOR SERVICE IN THE CONFEDERATE ARMY THAT A NEW FORCE OF RANGERS HAD BEEN RECRUITED FROM OLDER MEN AND BOYS.

COL. JOHN "RIP" FORD, RANGER COMMANDER

THE RANGERS, SERVING AS CONFEDERATE CAVALRY, HAD REPULSED EVERY ATTEMPT BY THE UNION ARMY TO MOVE UP THE RIO GRANDE.

FEARING THAT THE REBELS WOULD SURRENDER WHEN THEY LEARNED THE WAR WAS LOST, THE UNION COMMANDER ATTACKED THEIR CAMP TO GAIN PERSONAL GLORY IN THE LAST BATTLE OF THE WAR.

THE CONFEDERATES COUNTERATTACKED, ROUTED THE INVADERS, AND CHASED THEM SEVEN MILES BACK TO FORT BRAZOS ON THE COAST.

AFTER THE BATTLE THE CONFEDERATES LEARNED OF LEE'S SURRENDER, AND THEMSELVES SURRENDERED TO THE ARMY THEY HAD SO RECENTLY WHIPPED.

AND SO THE SOUTH HAD WON THE FIRST AND LAST BATTLES, BUT HAD LOST THE WAR.

THE HARD STRUGGLE FOR SOUTHERN INDEPENDENCE WAS OVER. THE STRUGGLE TO PRESERVE THE HONOR OF THE CONFEDERATE SOLDIER CONTINUES TO THIS DAY.

CHAPTER 20

RECONSTRUCTION
Woe to the Vanquished

ANDREW JOHNSON

WITH LINCOLN'S DEATH, VICE-PRESIDENT JOHNSON BECAME THE 17TH PRESIDENT OF THE UNITED STATES.

FORMER PRESIDENT JEFFERSON DAVIS WAS HELD IN SHACKLES IN A DANK FORTRESS CELL, AWAITING THE DECISION OF THE CONQUERERS.

IS THAT ALL THAT'S LEFT OF THE OLD TOWN?

YES, THEY CALL IT 'CHIMNEYVILLE' NOW!

VAST REGIONS OF THE SOUTH HAD BEEN DEVASTATED BY THE WAR. HOUSES, SCHOOLS, SOMETIMES WHOLE TOWNS HAD BEEN BURNED TO THE GROUND.

ONE OUT OF EVERY THREE CONFEDERATE SOLDIERS HAD DIED DURING THE WAR, AND MANY OF THE SURVIVORS WERE DISABLED.

HOW LONG IS AUNT RUBY GOING TO STAY, PA?

FROM NOW ON, ABNER, WITH HER HUSBAND DEAD AND HER HOUSE GONE SHE'S GOT NOWHERE ELSE TO GO.

THE RETURNING CONFEDERATE VETERAN HAD HEAVY RESPONSIBILITIES.

I'M GOING TO FOLLOW LINCOLN'S PLAN FOR RESTORING THE UNION.

IN MAY, 1865, PRESIDENT JOHNSON GRANTED AMNESTY TO MOST CONFEDERATE VETERANS, APPOINTED PROVISIONAL SOUTHERN STATE GOVERNMENTS AND HAD THEM HOLD ELECTIONS FOR NEW STATE AND FEDERAL OFFICES.

IT'S UNLAWFUL TO FORCE A STATE IN THIS WAY. BUT WE HAVE NO CHOICE!

SLAVERY IS A DEAD ISSUE ANYWAY!

LET'S GET BACK TO NORMAL!

AS A REQUIREMENT FOR REPRESENTATION IN CONGRESS. THE NEW STATE GOVERNMENTS RATIFIED THE 13TH AMENDMENT. ENDING SLAVERY EVERYWHERE IN THE U.S.A.

NEVER MIND WHAT THE PRESIDENT SAID! THE CONGRESS SAYS YOU WON'T BE SEATED UNTIL YOU RATIFY ANOTHER AMENDMENT!

BUT WHEN THE SOUTHERN STATES SENT THEIR NEWLY ELECTED SENATORS AND REPRESENTATIVES TO WASHINGTON. THE RADICAL REPUBLICANS REFUSED TO SEAT THEM.

IT LETS FORMER SLAVES VOTE BUT NOT OUR VETERANS!

IT KEEPS CONFEDERATE OFFICERS FROM ELECTIVE OFFICE!

IT MAKES OUR WAR BONDS WORTHLESS!

THE AMENDMENT IS DEFEATED!

THE RADICAL REPUBLICAN CONGRESS THEN DRAFTED THE 14TH AMENDMENT AND SENT IT TO THE STATES FOR RATIFICATION. THE NEW AMENDMENT WAS COMPLETELY UNACCEPTABLE TO THE SOUTH.

EACH STATE SHOULD DECIDE ITS OWN CITIZENSHIP QUALIFICATIONS!

KENTUCKY. CALIFORNIA. DELAWARE. AND MARYLAND JOINED THE SOUTHERN STATES IN OPPOSING THE NEW AMENDMENT.

THUNDERATION! WHAT CAN WE DO?

WE CAN FORCE THE SOUTHERN STATES TO CHANGE THEIR VOTES!

THE 14TH AMENDMENT DID NOT GET THE THREE-FOURTHS APPROVAL OF THE STATES REQUIRED FOR RATIFICATION. THE RADICAL REPUBLICNAS WERE FURIOUS.

IN ORDER TO GET THE 14TH AMENDMENT RATIFIED, CONGRESS PASSED THE RECONSTRUCTION ACT OF 1867. IT DECLARED THE SOUTHERN STATES TO BE NOT PART OF THE UNION.

THE NEW LAW DECLARED THE FORMER CONFEDERATE STATES TO BE OUTSIDE THE UNION UNTIL AND UNLESS THEY APPROVED THE 14TH AMENDMENT.

THE LAW DECLARED THE SOUTHERN STATES TO BE IN REBELLION. IT ESTABLISHED MARTIAL LAW. ONCE AGAIN A LARGE NORTHERN ARMY MOVED INTO THE SOUTH.

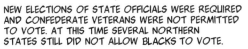

NEW ELECTIONS OF STATE OFFICIALS WERE REQUIRED AND CONFEDERATE VETERANS WERE NOT PERMITTED TO VOTE. AT THIS TIME SEVERAL NORTHERN STATES STILL DID NOT ALLOW BLACKS TO VOTE.

EVEN SOME OF THE NEWLY ELECTED STATE GOVERNMENTS REFUSED TO APPROVE THE 14TH AMENDMENT. THE GENERALS IN CHARGE DISMISSED LEGISLATURES THAT REFUSED TO CAVE IN.

BY THE TIME THE SOUTHERN STATES HAD BEEN FORCED TO APPROVE RATIFICATION OHIO, NEW JERSEY, AND WASHINGTON STATE HAD PASSED RESOLUTIONS WITHDRAWING THEIR PREVIOUS APPROVALS.

I PROCLAIM THAT: IF THE APPROVAL BY THE SOUTHERN STATES WAS LAWFUL, AND IF THE RESCISSIONS BY OTHER STATES IS UNLAWFUL THEN THE 14TH AMENDMENT IS RATIFIED.

RECOGNIZING THE ILLEGALITIES INVOLVED, SECRETARY OF STATE SEWARD ISSUED ONLY A QUALIFIED STATEMENT OF RATIFICATION.

CONGRESS THEN PASSED A RESOLUTION REQUIRING THE SECRETARY OF STATE TO GIVE AN UNQUALIFIED VERDICT OF RATIFICATION.

THE FOURTEENTH AMENDMENT WAS THEREFORE ENACTED, NOT TRULY RATIFIED.

NEVERTHELESS IT HAS BECOME THE BASIS FOR MANY SUBSEQUENT LAWS TRANSFERRING POWER FROM THE STATES TO THE CENTRAL GOVERNMENT.

RECONSTRUCTION: 1865 - 1877
THE TERM "RECONSTRUCTION" DID NOT REFER TO REBUILDING THE RAVAGES OF WAR. IT MEANT RESTRUCTURING THE SOUTHERN WAY OF LIFE.

NORTHERN OPPORTUNISTS FOLLOWED THE ARMY SOUTH HOPING TO MAKE MONEY OFF THE SUFFERING POPULATION. THEY WERE CALLED "CARPETBAGGERS" BECAUSE OF THEIR LUGGAGE MADE OF CARPET MATERIAL. THEY WERE JOINED BY TURNCOAT SOUTHERNERS CALLED "SCALAWAGS."

THE SOUTHERN VETERANS, WHO COULD NOT VOTE, WATCHED THE CARPETBAGGERS AND SCALAWAGS USE THE FORMER SLAVES TO ELECT CORRUPT STATE GOVERNMENTS.

THE FORMER SLAVES HAD LITTLE KNOWLEDGE OF CIVICS, ECONOMICS, OR LAW.

THE CARPETBAGGERS AND SCALAWAGS WERE THE REAL POWER BEHIND THE STATE GOVERNMENTS.

SOUTHERNERS WERE AT THE MERCY OF CORRUPT STATE GOVERNMENTS AND THE VENGEFUL FEDERAL GOVERNMENT.

THE BATTLE-HARDENED VETERANS WERE NOT ABOUT TO TAKE THIS EXPLOITATION LYING DOWN. THEY FORMED SECRET SOCIETIES TO INTIMIDATE THE FORMER SLAVES.

THE "NIGHT RIDERS" ALSO TARGETED THE SCALAWAGS AND CARPETBAGGERS.

PRESIDENT ULYSSES S. GRANT

ELECTED PRESIDENT IN 1868, HE ALLOWED THE CORRUPTION IN THE OCCUPIED STATES TO REACH INTO THE WHITEHOUSE. MILITARY RULE CONTINUED THROUGHOUT HIS TWO TERMS, BUT THE NORTHERN DEMOCRATS WERE MAKING A COMEBACK IN CONGRESS.

PRESIDENT RUTHERFORD B. HAYES

THE 1876 ELECTION WAS SO CLOSE IN THE ELECTORAL COLLEGE AND SO MANY VOTING IRREGULARITIES EXISTED THAT A COMPROMISE WAS REACHED. HAYES WAS DECLARED THE WINNER AFTER AGREEING TO END THE MILITARY OCCUPATION OF THE SOUTH.

TRUE TO HIS WORD, PRESIDENT HAYES ORDERED ALL TROOPS OUT OF THE SOUTH. RECONSTRUCTION WAS OVER. THE VETERANS COULD VOTE AGAIN. AND THE NIGHT RIDERS WERE DISBANDED.

ALL THE STATES, NOT JUST THE SOUTHERN, HAD LOST THEIR SOVEREIGNTY AS A RESULT OF THE WAR AND RECONSTRUCTION.

WITHOUT THE ABILITY TO SECEDE EACH STATE NOW HAD TO ACCEPT WHATEVER LAWS THE CENTRAL GOVERNMENT PASSED AND WHATEVER DECISIONS THE FEDERAL COURTS DECREED.

AMERICAN GRAMMAR CHANGED AS A RESULT OF THE WAR. AND "THE UNITED STATES" HAD CHANGED ITS MEANING FROM "THE UNITED NATIONS" TO "THE UNITED PROVINCES."

Surrender means that the history of this heroic struggle will be written by the enemy; that our youth will be trained by Northern school teachers; will learn from Northern school books their version of the War; will be impressed by all the influences of history and education to regard our gallant dead as traitors, and our maimed veterans as fit subjects for derision
-- General Pat Cleburne, CSA